THE GERMAN QUESTION

ROLF STEININGER

THE GERMAN QUESTION
THE STALIN NOTE OF 1952 AND THE PROBLEM OF REUNIFICATION

TRANSLATED BY JANE T. HEDGES
EDITED BY MARK CIOC

Columbia University Press
New York

Columbia University Press
New York   Oxford
The German Question: The Stalin Note of 1952 and the Problem of Reunification
is a translation of *Eine Vertane Chance. Die Stalin-Note vom 10. März 1952 und
die Wiedervereinigung* copyright © 1985 Verlag J. H. W. Dietz Nachf. GmbH,
Bonn, West Germany
Translation, foreword, preface, and notes copyright © 1990 Columbia University
Press

Library of Congress Cataloging-in-Publication Data

Steininger, Rolf, 1942–
[Vertane Chance. English]
The German question : the Stalin note of 1952 and the problem of
reunification / Rolf Steininger ; translated by Jane T. Hedges ;
edited by Mark Cioc.
p.   cm.
Includes bibliographical references and index.
ISBN 0-231-07216-3
1. German reunification question (1949–   )
2. German—Foreign relations—Soviet Union.
3. Soviet Union—Foreign relations—Germany.
4. Germany—History—Allied occupation, 1945–
5. Stalin, Joseph, 1879–1953.
I. Cioc, Mark. II. Title.
DD257.25.S776 1990   943.087—dc20   90-42116
                                          CIP

Casebound editions of Columbia University Press books are Smyth-sewn
and printed on permanent and durable acid-free paper

Printed in the United States of America
c 10 9 8 7 6 5 4 3 2 1

CONTENTS

v

Contents

DOCUMENTS

Documents

ABBREVIATIONS

CAB British Cabinet

CDU Christlich-Demokratische Union Deutschlands [Christian Democratic Union]

CSU Christlich-Soziale Union [Christian Social Union]

DoS U.S. Department of State

EDC European Defense Community

EU Europe

FDP Freie Demokratische Partei [Free Democratic Party]

FO British Foreign Office

FRG Federal Republic of Germany

FRUS *Foreign Relations of the United States*

Abbreviations

GDR   German Democratic Republic

KPD   Kommunistische Partei Deutschlands [Communist Party of Germany]

MAE   Ministère des Affaires Etrangères, Paris

NATO   North Atlantic Treaty Organization

PM   Prime Minister

PPS   Policy Planning Staff, U.S. Department of State

PREM   Prime Minister's Office

PRO   Public Record Office, London

PUSC   Permanent Under-Secretary of State (Sir William Strang) Committee

SED   Sozialistische Einheitspartei Deutschlands [Socialist Unity Party of Germany]

S/P   Policy Planning Staff, U.S. Department of State

SPD   Sozialdemokratische Partei Deutschlands [Social Democratic Party of Germany]

SRP   Sozialistische Reichspartei [Socialist Reich Party]

FOREWORD

In 1985, Rolf Steininger reopened a sensitive historical debate on German reunification. His timing was propitious, for at the same moment the Soviet Union embarked on a new era of perestroika and glasnost. With political reforms under way in East Germany, and the Wall no longer dividing Berlin, the "German question" has recaptured the limelight of international politics.

Did Western leaders miss an opportunity for German reunification in March 1952, when they refused to negotiate with Stalin? When Paul Sethe, the coeditor of the *Frankfurter Allgemeine Zeitung*, first raised this question in the mid-1950s, it provoked a divisive, and ultimately futile, debate over Stalin's intentions. The controversy subsided as West Germany became militarily integrated into the Western bloc, and as the three major West German political parties moved toward a tripartisan foreign policy in the 1960s. Yet, if the reunification issue receded temporarily from the purview of scholars, the mystery surrounding the Western response to the Stalin Note was never fully clarified. Why did Western leaders refuse to convoke a four-power conference, thereby leaving themselves open to the charge of missing an opportunity to settle the German problem?

Chancellor Konrad Adenauer's explanation has been frequently echoed by subsequent scholars: Western leaders viewed the Stalin Note as pure propaganda and therefore did not allow it to divert their attention from the task of ratifying the European Defense Community Treaty. This explanation has its merits. The timing, the content, and the public disclosure of the note all indicate that Stalin intended to mobilize public opinion in West Germany against the European Defense Community. There is, however, a circular logic to the official explanation: a conference failed to take place because the West concluded in advance that negotiations would end in failure. Nor is the government's argument altogether convincing. The negotiations over the European Defense Community, after all, had begun two years earlier and would continue for another two years, at which time French policy (not Soviet propaganda) undermined its success. Were there no moments to spare during those protracted negotiations when Western leaders might have discussed the Stalin Note with the Soviets?

After examining the newly opened British and American archival material in 1984, Professor Steininger realized that the Stalin Note episode was more complex than researchers had previously assumed. First, the West's initial response to the note was far from unanimous. British and American statesmen generally regarded the reunification offer as a sincere, albeit risky, solution to the German question. Both the U.S. State Department and the British Foreign Office expressed a willingness to convoke a four-power conference, in order to test Stalin's commitment to hold genuinely free all-German elections. Second, Chancellor Adenauer thwarted all negotiations with the Soviets—even negotiations based on free elections—because he distrusted his own people as much as he distrusted the governments of the Eastern bloc. In deference to Adenauer, Western leaders answered Stalin by initiating a propagandistic "battle of the notes," designed to help Adenauer win public support for Western integration, while feigning an interest in reunification. In 1953, the newly elected Prime Minister Winston Churchill announced that he would make a "solitary pilgrimage to Moscow" to seek a unified, neutralized Germany "if the Germans so wished." He learned firsthand what the State Department and the Foreign Office had realized a year earlier: Adenauer preferred Western integration to German reunification and therefore did not want the West to make any overtures to the Soviet Union.

Professor Steininger's critics accused him of "utopianism," of spreading a "missed-opportunity" myth, and of creating a new "stab-in-the-back" legend. Yet they could not dispute the fact that he had meticulously accumulated an overwhelming amount of archival evidence to support his conclusions: Adenauer's central role in the formulation of Western policy toward the Stalin Note is now indisputable.

This translation will make Professor Steininger's work more accessible to the Anglo-American scholarly community. Few historical problems can lay claim to greater contemporary importance than the question of German reunification.

Mark Cioc
University of California, Santa Cruz

PREFACE

The present study first appeared as the introduction to the documentary collection *Eine Chance zur Wiedervereinigung?*[1] The documentation took a long time to assemble. Under the Freedom of Information Act, the American documents were made available in 1980. But a publication based solely on American archival sources seemed to make little sense, given that the British had played an equally important role in handling the Stalin Note, as indeed they had in formulating all Western policy toward Germany since 1945.[2] Once the British documents became available in 1983, it was clear that waiting had been worthwhile.

This book aims to provide a solid basis for discussing one of the most controversial, difficult, and important chapters of German postwar history and to remove it from the usual realm of speculation. Readers can reevaluate the findings presented here and make their own judgments about what really occurred. What impressions, goals, and considerations motivated the Western powers and Konrad Adenauer in their "policy toward reunification"? To what extent can one justifiably continue to speak of the "myth of the missed opportunity"? To what extent is Adenauer's premise true, "that we will only attain Germany's reunification with the help of the three Western allies, never with the help of the Soviet Union"?

In May 1955, almost ten years to the day after the capitulation, occupation ended for the West German state. The Federal Republic became conditionally sovereign and a member of NATO. The perpetuation of Germany's division was the price paid. Whether this price was not perhaps too high, whether indeed another path for German history did not exist that would have been worth pursuing (or at least exploring) in the interests of German unity—these concerns formed the theme of bitter controversies in the early years of the republic. The astoundingly successful history of the Federal Republic in the following years did not end this controversy but only hid it from view. The arguments of Adenauer's critics have lost nothing of their validity even today. A younger generation has begun anew to discuss the old questions and controversies. And the more documents from the 1950s that become available, the more solid will be the basis on which this debate can be conducted. If the evidence I have gathered gives a new impulse to the discussion of this topic, and if possibly new answers can be given to the old questions, then much will have been gained and it will have been worth the effort.

I would like to thank the following people: the officials in the Department of State in Washington, D.C., and in the Eisenhower Library in Abilene, Kansas, who helped me overcome so many of the obstacles on my way to the documents; the employees in the Public Record Office in London, especially Mr. C. D. Chalmers, head of the Search Department, who always had time for my questions and whose assistance in deciphering many individuals' handwriting was invaluable; the Keeper of Public Records for permission to reprint the documents; Mrs. Angela Houston, who provided research assistance; Sir Frank Roberts, head of the German section in the Foreign Office from 1951 to 1954 for a fascinating, open talk about British policy toward Germany; my secretary, Fräulein Anita Goestl, for deciphering my handwriting; my assistants, Dr. Thomas Albrich and Mag. Klaus Eisterer—who also conducted research in Paris—for their help in reading the galley proofs; the editorial staff of the Archiv für Sozialgeschichte for including this work in their series; and especially to both Herr Dr. Dieter Dowe, whose great commitment benefited this project from its inception, and the editorial secretary, Frau Holde Schwarz, for her patience and constant helpfulness.

My work on this documentation occurred during a move from Hannover to Innsbruck; nevertheless, my wife oversaw my return to my study with the same degree of forbearance she always shows. Thus, I dedicate this book to her—for Eva.

THE GERMAN QUESTION

CHAPTER ONE

THE STALIN NOTE AND
GERMAN SCHOLARSHIP
The Historiographic Debate

On March 10, 1952, the Soviet deputy foreign minister, Andrei Gromyko, delivered a note to the delegates of the three Western powers in Moscow. The Soviet government proposed, among other things, to

1. Reestablish Germany as a unified state within the boundaries "established by the provisions of the Potsdam Conference."

2. Obligate Germany "not to enter into any kind of coalition or military alliance directed against any power which took part with its armed forces in the war against Germany."

3. Withdraw all occupying forces by, at the latest, one year following the effective date of the peace treaty, the preparation of which was to involve a unified German government.

4. Allow Germany to have "its own national armed forces (land, air, and sea) which are necessary for the defense of the country."

5. Permit Germany to manufacture its own munitions for these armed forces.

6. Refrain from restricting Germany's nonmilitary economy, trade, shipping, and access to world markets.

7. Allow the free activity of democratic political parties and organizations.

8. Grant all former members of the German army and the Nazis (with the exception of convicted war criminals) the right to equal participation in the establishment of a peaceful, democratic Germany.[1]

Not only did the "Stalin Note" and the subsequent exchange of diplomatic notes lead to passionate discussions among contemporaries, but these notes remain today the object of controversy—usually with strong emotional overtones—among politicians, historians, and journalists. As the last bungled opportunity for reunification, the Stalin Note has "sunk itself deep into the collective subconscious of an entire generation," remarked Hans-Peter Schwarz at a meeting of the Konrad Adenauer Foundation in Rhöndorf on March 26, 1981.[2] At the same meeting, Arnulf Baring alluded to the long-term effect of this note: "We have not yet managed to escape from this March note and we will not be able to do so. . . . The question is not history. . . . We are concerned here with a topical issue that will remain topical until the Germans come to terms with their own national identity."[3]

This situation is not surprising since what is at issue is the question of who bears the responsibility for the continuing division of Germany.

In 1956, the problem of the "forfeited opportunity" came sharply to the public's attention when Paul Sethe (coeditor of the *Frankfurter Allgemeine Zeitung* until 1955) published a book, *Zwischen Bonn und Moskau* (Between Bonn and Moscow), in which he spoke of the "missed opportunity."[4] (Back in 1952, Sethe had vehemently demanded negotiations with the Soviet Union, but he saw no further chance for reunification after the Federal Republic was integrated into the Western alliance.) The assertion of the "missed opportunity" was raised anew on January 23, 1958, in the famous Bundestag debate between Thomas Dehler (Free Democratic Party [FDP], Minister of Justice in Adenauer's cabinet in 1952) and Gustav Heinemann (Minister of the Interior in Adenauer's cabinet until 1950 and Federal President from 1969 to 1974), which lasted until the early hours of the morning. Dehler and Heinemann thus put themselves at the center of the storm over Adenauer's policies concerning reunification.[5] This was "probably the most vehement and passionate verbal battle that this parliament had yet experienced."[6] Since then, this issue has never been laid to rest. Numerous publications have dealt with it, but essentially the same questions keep reappearing:

1. How "serious" was the Soviet offer, that is, what intentions lay behind Joseph Stalin's initiative? Were the Kremlin leaders at that time prepared to alter their policy toward Germany? Was it in their interest to agree to a unified and militarily nonaligned Germany?

2. During the negotiations involving the Soviet note, what were the impressions, goals, and considerations of the Western powers that, in the end, led them to reject the Soviet offer? How great was the contradiction between public pronouncements, such as the obligation to reunification assumed under the terms of the Bonn Convention, and private thoughts?

3. What role did Adenauer play in the formulation of the Western powers' policy toward the note? What considerations motivated him at the time? Did he see a "chance for reunification" in Stalin's offer? What priority did reunification actually hold in his policy? Was his publicly presented formula—that integration into the Western alliance constituted the shortest path to reunification—*the* great lie of the 1950s? How accurate was his equation "Neutralization means sovietization"?[7] Was the issue "freedom versus slavery" as he maintained? To what extent was he responsible for the failure to fully explore the ramifications of the note, and thus for the continuing division of Germany?

4. How much latitude did the Germans have? Could Soviet intentions have been clarified at the negotiating table without endangering the existing policy of integrating the Federal Republic into the Western camp? In other words, could the note have been handled differently so that, as the prominent Social Democrat Carlo Schmid stated in his *Erinnerungen* (Memoirs), at least "some friends of the fatherland who are today concerned about Germany's future would be spared the nostalgic glance backward to 1952"?[8]

When we look at the numerous publications about the Stalin Note, it is remarkable with what decisiveness such authors as Hans Buchheim, Jürgen Weber, Wolfgang Wagner, and Gerhard Wettig have taken the view,[9] with no documents at hand, that it is a myth to speak of a missed opportunity. In their view, the Soviet Union was by no means prepared to alter its policy toward Germany in the spring of 1952. The Soviet Union supported a four-power conference, but solely with the intent of gaining some time through protracted negotiations in order to delay, and if possible to prevent, the establishment of a European Defense Community and the consequent rearmament of the Federal Republic. In other words, the Stalin Note was merely a deceptive and disruptive maneuver by the Soviets.

Even if this were *one* of the Soviet Union's goals—and the decisive test was never made—other historians have presented equally good arguments supporting the opposite position. Thus, very early on, Boris Meissner expounded the view that the Soviets' initiative in large measure revealed their willingness to consider German national interests and to achieve an orderly relationship with the West.[10] Rather than a tactical maneuver, it was a substantive part of a disengagement concept that Stalin developed (with L. P. Beria's and G. M. Malenkov's help) but that failed to find the necessary domestic support. To bolster this argument Meissner cites:

1. The Soviet attempts during 1951–52 to create a zone of neutral states designed to separate East and West.

2. Stalin's conviction that Germany and Japan would make a comeback and that conflict within the capitalist world was inevitable, as expressed in his work "Economic Problems of Socialism in the USSR" in February 1952. Strengthening these two nations was in the Soviet interest according to this view, since their strength would lessen the possibility of a war between East and West.

3. Stalin's suggestion of long-term coexistence to avoid a world war. The term *peaceful coexistence* was first used by Beria on November 6, 1951, and then by Stalin on March 31, 1952, long before Nikita Khrushchev popularized it.

4. The "decisive" fact that "Beria's and Malenkov's constructive policy toward Germany, pursued from the autumn of 1951 to the spring of 1952, was promptly resumed when they briefly assumed power after Stalin's death on March 5, 1953."

According to this view, the hardening of the Soviet attitude toward the German question, which is noticeable in the third Soviet note of May 1952 (see chapter 8) is attributable less to the impending signing of the European Defense Community Treaty and the Bonn Convention than to the shift of power in the Kremlin. As a result of the purges in Georgia and the change at the top of the Ministry for State Security in the autumn of 1952, Beria's position was weakened, Khrushchev's strengthened. Without exploring Meissner's argument under Point 4 above, Richard Löwenthal[11] has concluded that the real opportunity for solving the German question first arose in the months between Stalin's death and June 17, 1953, and that this opportunity was in fact bungled. (This position will be explored further in chapter 10.)

Klaus Erdmenger and, in a somewhat different manner, Gerd Meyer[12] are convinced that the Soviet offer was, as Meyer put it, "at least partially" serious: in the medium and long run, it offered more advantages than disadvantages to the Soviet Union. Accordingly, the Soviets were prepared to pay a high price to prevent the establishment of the European Defense Community and to neutralize Germany, even though the exact details of Germany's neutrality were yet to be negotiated.

We should again clarify under that conditions the Soviet offer was made. In the autumn of 1950, as a result of the Korean conflict, the United States exerted extreme pressure on Great Britain and, especially, France to agree in principle to the rearmament of West Germany to ensure the effective defense of Western Europe. The attainment of this objective, however, met with enormous difficulties, the sources of which were to be found primarily in Paris. The idea of German soldiers, whether in the uniform of a European army or, even worse, in German uniform, was slow to gain acceptability in France, especially since by 1951 the danger of a global war stemming from the Korean conflict seemed to have subsided.

Even though the negotiations to establish the European Defense Community turned out to be extremely troublesome, by early 1952 their successful conclusion was in sight: the Federal Republic would provide twelve divisions for the army, a tactical air force of 85,000 men (1,300 airplanes), and 12,000 naval troops for a total of approximately 400,000 men—making it on paper the second largest army in Western Europe. In fact, it would be the largest, since a large part of the French army was fighting in Indochina. The formation of the German contingents as an integral part of a Western military force was to take place as quickly as possible, preferably by the end of 1952. These troops would be recruited from the ranks of soldiers with "Russian experience," those who had fought near Leningrad and Moscow. In the "Great Patriotic War," the Russians had repulsed the German aggressors only with an incredible loss of life—and with the support of the Americans. Now the German military potential would be on the side of the United States.

To this already menacing constellation was added the atomic superiority of the United States and the decision by the North Atlantic Treaty Organization (NATO) ministers' council at its meeting in Lisbon from February 20 to 25, 1952, to include Turkey and Greece in NATO, to form a Middle East detachment for NATO, and to raise an army in Western Europe of 100 divisions by the end of 1954, half of which would be combat-ready. In the Kremlin's view, this development had to be halted; on March 10, Stalin set the price. There was a deeper meaning behind this date: exactly thirteen years before, on March 10, 1939, in his speech before the Eighteenth Communist Party Congress, he had announced a completely unanticipated change in German–Soviet relations [with the Hitler–Stalin Pact in August 1939].

Yet another point must be kept in mind. Although Stalin had described the founding of the German Democratic Republic (GDR) as a "turning point in the history of Europe," the GDR developed into a sort of burdensome mortgage for the Kremlin. Enormous domestic difficulties confronted the GDR leaders. In an attempt to forge the GDR into the bulwark of socialism, the productive infrastructure and the workers had been so severely overtaxed that the resulting economic and social misery actually endangered the regime's existence. A significant heavy industrial base was to be conjured up without regard for the difficulties of a country weakened by war and demolition, and with few raw materials of its own. For example, in 1936, 1.2 million tons of raw steel were produced on the territory now comprising the GDR; in 1946, only 97,000 tons. The planned goal for 1955 called for 3.4 million tons. This could be accomplished only at the expense of the consumer goods industry, and the result was a further decline in the standard of living. In addition, thousands of peasants preferred fleeing to the West over accepting forced collectivization in "agricultural cooperatives" (in 1951, 4,343 fled without family members; in 1952, 14,141; in 1953, 37,396). In 1952, 13 percent of the arable land lacked someone to cultivate it. The "intensification of the class struggle" led to an increase in refugees among other professional groups as well. In the first six months of 1952, 72,226 refugees were registered; in the second six months of 1952, 110,167 people fled; and from January to May 1953, 184,793 people left the GDR.

"In such a situation," as Wilfried Loth of Essen University stated, "sacrificing SED [Socialist Unity Party] control of the GDR might seem a reasonable price to pay to prevent the West's superiority in the cold war."[13] He is thus in agreement not only with Boris Meissner, but also with Andreas Hillgruber, who observed in his stringent analysis "Adenauer und die Stalin-Note vom März 1952" (Adenauer and the Stalin Note of March 1952) that today "one can hardly continue to dispute that the note reflected Stalin's serious interest in neutralizing Germany." Stalin assumed as he had between the two world wars, that tensions existed between the "imperialist" powers (as can be gathered from Stalin's "Economic Problems of Socialism in the USSR") and that it was in the Soviet Union's interest to promote these tensions. (Löwenthal, too, sees Stalin's foreign policy during the last year of his life as primarily oriented toward inflaming conflicts between the Western powers.) In this framework, enabling Germany to go its own way assumed central importance. Hillgruber also believed that Stalin was prepared to pay a very high price, "even to abandon the GDR and the SED," to prevent Germany's military potential from being integrated into the Western alliance, since this was considered especially dangerous: "In Stalin's view, a neutralized unified Germany (although by force of circumstances one with a bourgeois structure), whose status was guaranteed by the Western powers including the United States, was more acceptable than a Germany integrated into the Western alliance as provided for by the Western treaties."[14]

As distinguished as most of the existing works on the Stalin Note are, new facts or essentially new discoveries of great import have not been brought to light since 1952 either by contemporary witnesses or by historians. Many investigations have suffered because the documents of the participating governments were not accessible. Thus it is significant that Hermann Graml of the Institut für Zeitgeschichte in Munich was the first German historian to examine a portion of the American documents. In a lengthy article written in 1977, Graml had attacked the view that the note was a constructive offer.[15] Even after examining the American documents, he concluded that the Stalin Note remains the "myth of the missed opportunity." He proceeded from the assertion that the notes stem from Stalin's recognition that the Federal Republic's integration into the Western alliance and the development of the European Defense Community had become inevitable. He summed up his most important conclusions as follows:

1. At no time during 1952 did the Soviet Union propose reunification under acceptable conditions, namely, by agreeing to sacrifice SED control to permit free elections throughout a unified Germany. Instead, the Soviet Union wanted to regain the initiative in the propaganda war and, "by conveniently laying the blame at the West's door," facilitate the firm establishment of the GDR as a member of the Soviet bloc as well as lend support to Western opponents of Western European integration.

2. The government and chancellor of the Federal Republic exercised only minimal influence over the Western powers' stance toward the note, even though during the exchange of notes the Federal Republic's position unquestionably improved.

3. For these reasons, there is no validity in the assertion that "a

chance for reunification was mishandled in 1952, especially based on the behavior of the federal chancellor."[16]

Graml first presented the results of this research at the 1981 meeting in Rhöndorf. How deeply concern about Adenauer's having warded off any exploration of the Soviet note was rooted even in Christian Democratic Union (CDU) minds could be seen by the appreciation shown Graml's argument. Bundestag President Eugen Gerstenmaier's appreciation was especially enthusiastic. In his appearance at universities, he had frequently been forced to reply to the question: Why did you pass up this opportunity? At the National Synod of the German Protestant Church, of which he was a prominent member, he repeatedly responded to this question from a "well-nigh wounded soul": "For many years I myself have been unsure whether we reacted properly, especially to the first Stalin Note, not to the later ones." Graml's presentation freed Gerstenmaier from these "conflicting feelings." With thanks to Graml and in a voice filled with emotion, he directed the above words to his party colleague Johann B. Gradl (chairman of the exiled East German CDU), raising his hand imploringly as though trying to ward off temptation. For Gradl had refocused the discussion on the heart of the matter and had remonstrated Graml: The discussion was not of a missed opportunity, that was not the issue. Instead, the question was whether the opportunity had been fully explored, and whether "this exploration had not been undertaken with due seriousness."

Stephen G. Thomas, Kurt Schumacher's close confidante and the former head of the eastern desk of the Social Democratic Party (SPD), took up Meissner's and Hillgruber's considerations mentioned above and shifted the focus away from complaints about West Germany's allies and toward the Kremlin once again. (At the Rhöndorf meeting, Thomas again emphasized that in his opinion the Soviets were concerned not merely with circumventing the European Defense Community but also with attaining "something completely different.") In his view, the note was a "legitimate element of Soviet pressure politics . . . , a genuine concern of Soviet diplomacy and power strategy at this strategic juncture in the spring of 1952."[17]

In support of this theory, Thomas quoted from SED chief Walter Ulbricht's speech to the SED District Delegates' Conference in Leipzig on May 28, 1960:

I will openly state that our proposal of 1952 contained a certain risk for the GDR as well, for the workers. At that time the GDR was not as well anchored and the entire population did not have as clear-cut a view of the issues of safeguarding the peace, reunification, and the character of West German authority as they do now. But we were prepared to conduct the battle on an open field.[18] That would have meant a long battle in Germany.

Thomas interprets this statement as follows: "The Soviet Union's power interests prevailed over the particular interests of the SED; Stalin would have thrown Ulbricht overboard in the controversy concerning a unified Germany. This was the concern that Ulbricht confirmed many years later."[19]

Thomas also offered a second document, an interview with the leader of the Italian socialists, Pietro Nenni, in the *New York Times* on March 26, 1963. In response to this interview, GDR President Wilhelm Pieck and Prime Minister Otto Grotewohl both explained: "At that time, in 1952, Stalin wanted to put us in a new situation and we do not know how we would have got out of it!"[20]

Gerd Bucerius, a CDU member of the Bundestag in 1952 and for many years the editor of *Die Zeit*, described what he considered the greatly limited field on which German policy could maneuver:

On the one side [was] a treaty ready to be signed [the European Defense Community Treaty and the Bonn Convention], and on the other side, a . . . very slight hope. . . . The difficulty was that at the moment we entered into negotiations with the Soviet Union, the West would have run away, and we would have been thrown upon the mercy of the Soviets. . . . Within the course of a few days we had to decide: with the West or with the East. We decided to go with the West.[21]

In the *Frankfurter Allgemeine Zeitung* on the thirtieth anniversary of the Stalin Note on March 10, 1982, Wilhelm Grewe once again took a position on the "tenacious myth" of the note and on the "error of the missed opportunity for German reunification." In his editorial, he vehemently attacked Gradl's reproach, made at the Rhöndorf meeting, that the note was dismissed without a serious attempt to "plumb the depths" of the Soviet initiative. His thesis: Adenauer could not have behaved any differently. He describes as "completely unrealistic" the idea that the Bonn government could have first inquired in Moscow or demanded a four-power conference without wrecking the treaties with the West.

What possibilities existed in his view? He rejects "sending emissaries to Moscow" or "meeting secretly with the Soviet ambassador in the capital city of a third country without informing the West" as "risky ideas." This argument seems persuasive, and this course would indeed have been risky, but Grewe fails to mention that these were not the only possibilities; consequently, the questions are incorrectly posed. Other possibilities did in fact exist, and they will be thoroughly examined later (see chapters 4 and 7). But Grewe even rejects the "officially correct approach" of asking the Western occupying powers "to use their ambassadors in Moscow to explore the issue": "The answer is superfluous."[22] Nevertheless, a third possibility still existed: Should the Bonn government have urged the Western powers to convene a four-power conference? In his talk in Rhöndorf, Eugen Gerstenmaier pointed out that this "lay within our possibilities." His similar suggestion to Adenauer received the following response:

> If we do that, if we force the issue, do you know what the result will be? The result will be that we will sit between two chairs in the end. Absolutely nothing will change in the East; even long, long negotiations will reveal that this was only a stratagem. The effect in the West will be the refrain, "The Germans are only fair-weather friends." In short, we will be sitting between two chairs.[23]

Grewe shared his opinion and his metaphor: "The prospect of tangible results would be minimal; the risk of falling amongst all the chairs would be maximal."[24] That the situation was probably not this simple can be seen from the following. Grewe hit upon the heart of the matter when he posed the question: What would have induced Adenauer to jeopardize the imminent inclusion of the Federal Republic in the Western alliance, since Adenauer considered a neutralized Germany—in whatever form—to be a calamity (on this point, see chapter 2). As Grewe again emphatically stated at the "Aschaffenburg talks" of 1984, in Adenauer's view there was no alternative to integration into the Western alliance; before the treaties with the West were signed and ratified, there was nothing to negotiate and thus no reason to explore the ramifications of the note.

Now additional American and, for the first time, British documents are available that shed more light on this note. Let me say at the start that these documents offer no corroboration to proponents of the "myth" school of thought, nor do they substantiate Graml's theses. Even if they fail to provide final, definitive proof of the "seriousness" of the Soviet offer, they certainly answer a great number of the questions posed above. Above all, they reveal what considerations were motivating the

Western powers during the negotiations concerning the note, what role Adenauer played, and what latitude existed on the German side—that is, what would have been possible.

The British documents offer at least a hint of Stalin's intentions. On July 26, 1952, the Russian dictator spoke with Pietro Nenni, the leader of the Italian left socialists, while Nenni was at the Kremlin to receive the peace prize. Nenni, who was at that time a proponent of close cooperation with the Communists, told the Italian ambassador to Moscow, Baron Mario di Stefano, about his conversation with Stalin immediately thereafter. Di Stefano then passed his information along to the Canadian ambassador. What he reported wound up in a secret telegram to the British Foreign Office—via a detour through Ottawa—where it lay under lock and key for thirty years. According to these sources, Stalin had explained that with the first note the Politburo was "really willing to make sacrifices to obtain unification." They would have sacrificed the East German Communists so as to bring about a Germany ruled by a government friendly to the West, but containing a strong leftist opposition, as in Italy.

Stalin believed that a weak Germany with strong political forces looking to both the West and the Soviet Union would bring about a political equilibrium sufficient to stop any drift to war. The Politburo realized that reunification had become impossible and that two Germanys must continue to exist after the European Defense Community Treaty and the Bonn Convention were signed by the Western powers and ratified by the U.S. Senate, and after Dwight D. Eisenhower was nominated as a presidential candidate—from which Stalin concluded that Eisenhower would become the next president. Stalin then decided to establish a military balance between West and East by matching the strength of the NATO forces in West Germany with an equally strong East German army. From that time on, he expected that the split between the two Germanys would continue for some time, but he felt that there would be no war as long as there was a strong East Germany under Soviet control to protect Russia's western flank. Stalin saw Germany no longer as the supreme danger spot, but as just another area where the Soviet Union's long-range goals had to be pursued. The exchange of notes had lost its significance.[25]

In another work, I concluded that this telegram substantiated the view of those who refuse to dismiss the note as a deceptive and disruptive maneuver and who especially refer to Meissner and Hillgruber.[26] But elsewhere this interpretation was rejected. Gerd Bucerius, on the basis of Nenni's memoirs, remarked emphatically in *Die Zeit:* "[There is] not a word about the Stalin Note. For Nenni's readers, however, this would have been a momentous disclosure."[27]

Indeed, Nenni does not mention the note in his diaries (and certainly not Stalin's reference to Eisenhower).[28] He even disclaimed comments alluding to this conversation in his party organ *Avanti* on August 10, 1952. One can only speculate on his reasons, since, on the other hand, a few weeks later, he discussed his conversation with Stalin in a three-hour interview with Richard Crossman, a British journalist and representative of the opposition Labour Party.

Crossman published a summary on September 20, 1952, in the socialist weekly *New Statesman and Nation.*[29] This seemed important enough to the *Frankfurter Allgemeine Zeitung,* whose coeditor at that time was Paul Sethe, to take a position on the matter in an editorial "Was hat Stalin gesagt?" (What Did Stalin Say?) on September 24, 1952: "Since we cannot know whether Nenni correctly reported Stalin's thoughts, and since we can be even less clear about the goals Stalin was pursuing through his conversation with the Italian socialist, we report the essence of Crossman's report with all due reservations." According to this report, Nenni had the clear impression that the first Russian note constituted a serious offer, but that Stalin then abandoned the hope of a four-power conference at which Germany would be reunified by agreement and viewed the continuing division of Germany with equanimity. In addition, Stalin was supposed to have reassured Nenni that he would do everything to avoid provocation. The Kremlin was said to be quite skeptical of the idea of dividing the Atlantic Alliance and, especially, of driving a wedge between the United States and Great Britain. Nevertheless, Stalin would not consider relinquishing any territory in Eastern Europe that he had acquired in 1945 merely to appease the Americans. Nenni's general impression was that neither a catastrophe nor a peaceful settlement was imminent. The twilight between war and peace would persist indefinitely, and we had to accept that.

To dismiss all this as pure speculation and "overinterpretation" is too simple. Bucerius points to a possible error in transmitting the telegram mentioned above and then continues: "But let's assume for a moment that Stalin really did speak with Nenni about the note. Would he have been able to say that he was not serious about the note, that he only wanted to disrupt the negotiations concerning the Bonn Convention? Only to quickly add that his maneuver had been unsuccessful?"[30]

Wilhelm Grewe presented this argument at the "Aschaffenburg talks" in 1984. What answers are there to these questions? It is indeed striking that Stalin referred expressly to the first note and then clearly stated that reunification would become impossible after the treaties with the Western powers were signed. Many in the West foresaw this result of the treaties, and some feared it. It would have been much more cunning for Stalin to continue to affirm Soviet readiness for reunification in the interest of a deceptive and disruptive maneuver, rather than to deny the usefulness or a further exchange of notes.[31]

Now, as before, I consider this telegram an expression of Stalin's intentions. It is, of course, not a protocol from a Politburo meeting; nonetheless Walter Laqueur[32] fails to convince me when he simply asserts that the interview between Stalin and Nenni proves "nothing" because Stalin was not in the habit of taking even his closest collaborators into his confidence, let along foreign Communists, let alone foreigners who were not even Communists. Why would the Italian ambassador di Stefano relate something that was not true? I can find no tactical reason on his part, since there was nothing he could hope to influence.

Although Laqueur insists that the history of Soviet–German relations did not end with the third Soviet note in May 1952, the lack of progress on the German question until after Stalin's death challenges that assertion. And when he maintains that, in later years, the Soviets had countless opportunities to prove their willingness to make concessions, we must remind him that the problem encountered in 1952 remained exactly the same in subsequent years: the West refused to budge an inch from its position and essentially demanded the Soviets' capitulation. When Laqueur deplored the West's failure to explore the seriousness of Stalin's proposal—not in the hope of achieving a "sensational breakthrough," but for the historical record in order to forestall the mythology of "missed opportunities"—then he should at least have explored the motive underlying this attitude. This he did not do. If he had, he would have needed to point out the discrepancy between public statements, such as the Western powers' commitment to reunification made in the Bonn Convention, and private thoughts (see chapter 6).

In support of his "alibi theory," Hermann Graml quotes a Soviet diplomat active in London who let slip to a Swiss colleague at the beginning of May that in Moscow they did not anticipate the acceptance of the Soviet proposals; the note campaign was only staged to help stabilize the GDR.[33] But we must compare the report made by the deputy French ambassador to Washington, J. Daridan, on June 28. Vladykin, second counselor at the Soviet embassy, spoke to two colleagues at the French embassy about various political problems. The report to the Quai d'Orsay reads as follows:

First of all, concerning the German question, Mr. Vladykin explained that he was surprised the allies were so concerned to establish rigorous precautionary measures before general elections were held in Germany. The Western zone, he said, contains more than two-thirds of the German population. The Eastern zone is far from being uniformly communist. In general elections the Communists would represent only a small minority in the national assembly. The government resulting from such elections would necessarily be oriented toward the West. Even if one accepts that conditions in East Germany are not what one could wish for, they present no danger at all.

When one of my colleagues asked him why Russia would propose a solution with so many disadvantages for Russia itself, Mr. Vladykin responded that precisely these considerable concessions prove the fairness of the Russian proposals. Moscow is prepared to accept that Germany will have a non-Communist, even an anti-Communist, government in order to attain two goals in compensation: the first is the end of the division of Germany, a division that carries within itself the danger of a world war; the second is the neutralization of Germany.

In response, my colleagues remarked that it is not enough to decide that Germany will become neutral for it to remain neutral. It is certainly possible to include guarantees to this end in the text and, especially, to limit the national army Germany is to have at its disposal; but solutions of this sort are always fragile, as experience with the Treaty of Versailles has shown. The Soviet diplomat confined himself to the answer that for the Soviet government it is significant that Germany is not authorized to join any alliance and did not discuss the effectiveness of a neutrality forced upon Germany. Even united, Germany would no longer be in the position to wage war alone. Germany could only carry out an aggressive action with the support of one of the two great powers. On the other hand, a great power outside of Europe, such as the United States, could only with difficulty conduct a European campaign against Russia without the help of Germany. The diligence with which the government of the United States has endeavored to bring Germany to its side and to rearm Germany appears to the Soviets as one of the most alarming signs of the United States' intentions.

By way of these comments, Mr. Vladykin came to speak of the

fear American policy has created in Moscow. In this connection he referred to the foreign policy program recently developed by [John] Foster Dulles, who recommends a more active policy than that of "containment" for the United States. He highlighted the explanations Mr. [Dean] Acheson offered in response to Mr. Dulles, in which Acheson underscored the dynamic character of his own diplomacy. [Vladykin] alluded to various trends in public opinion that could be summarized under the heading "policy of repression." In conclusion, he felt that in the long run the highest goal of United States' foreign policy was to bring about a change of regime in the USSR one way or another.

My colleagues suggested that one must consider the influence of domestic policy when explaining [the behavior of] American politicians, especially in an election year; that a widespread aversion to any idea of aggression exists in the United States; that even in Communist regimes in countries behind the iron curtain or even in Russia itself some authorized voices express sympathy for the opposition, yet this open hostility toward the Communist regime does not necessarily indicate the intention of falling back on the use of force. As far as American desires to achieve Germany's participation in Western defense are concerned, they stem not from the aggressive intentions of the United States but from the desire to make Europe capable of defending itself and, in the long run, to reduce the burden of stationing American troops abroad. Mr. Vladykin, who throughout the entire conversation remained moderate and objective (although the opportunity was frequently there, he never contended that the South Koreans were responsible for the attack last June, nor that America had used bacteriological weapons, nor that the East German regime was completely democratic), acknowledged that there was no proof of the aggressive intentions of the United States. Nevertheless, he could not help but believe that the attitude of the United States would justify the fears of his government.[34]

Naturally, one can dismiss even these remarks as pure propaganda, but to do so would be to oversimplify the matter. Even in 1984, Gerd Bucerius still saw no opportunity in the note; he used the former Austrian chancellor, Bruno Kreisky, as a witness who had asked Foreign Minister V. M. Molotov in 1954 if a settlement such as that reached for Austria would not be possible for Germany. As Kreisky told Bucerius, Molotov rejected even the arrangements that Stalin had proposed in 1952: "The Germans occupied our country twice by force of arms. Austria's neutrality can be secured with a piece of paper. Germany's neutrality cannot."[35]

This famous argument, which rejects a similarity between the German and the Austrian situation, certainly carries some weight. But—disregarding for the moment to what extent Bruno Kreisky can be considered the final authority on Soviet policy toward Germany—the situation in 1954 did not even faintly resemble that strategic juncture, that unique constellation encountered in the spring of 1952. This fact is probably overlooked by those who believe that absolutely nothing was lost by signing the treaties with the Western powers. If the Soviets were serious, this argument goes, they could have proved it at the foreign ministers' conference in January–February 1954.[36] (But those who so argue also conceal the fact that the West's position had not changed at all.)

However, by 1954, the situation for the Soviet Union had changed fundamentally. The West was further than ever from implementing the NATO decision made in Lisbon (100 divisions), the feared German soldiers were nowhere to be seen, and only visionaries still believed in the ratification of the European Defense Community Treaty—certainly not anyone in the Kremlin. Strategically (with the long-range bomber) the Soviet Union had gained parity (according to Central Intelligence Agency [CIA] estimates), and in the autumn of 1953, the Soviet Union had also completed development of the hydrogen bomb. Moreover, the chances for a negotiated settlement of the German question acceptable to the Soviets had been proved to be slight in 1953. The first steps had unleashed a crisis, potentially endangering the entire Soviet Eastern European empire: as of June 17, 1953, the GDR was no longer expendable; on the contrary, the Ulbricht regime required shoring up.

Bucerius, like many others, has doubted the soundness of his decision in the spring of 1952 not to press more strongly for negotiations. On October 12, 1972, he made a further attempt at explanation and asked George F. Kennan, the American ambassador in Moscow in 1952, whether the CDU's and the Christian Social Union's (CSU) concerns ("about falling amongst all the chairs") were justified "or whether Kennan would have advised us at that time to await the results of the negotiations with the Soviet Union and then to ratify" (*sign* is clearly meant here). On December 2, 1972, Kennan gave a short but characteristic answer:

> The issue you mention arose not just in 1952 but, as a matter of
> principle, on other occasions as well: in 1949, in connection with

the so-called contractuals, and again in 1957, in connection with the decision to base the Western European NATO defenses on the "tactical" nuclear weapons, and above all in the decision, in 1954–55, to bring Western Germany into NATO and to re-arm it as a part of NATO.

What Dr. Adenauer never seemed to understand was that each of these steps, while given precedence over negotiations with Russia and defended on the grounds that they would strengthen Germany's position in such negotiations, actually foreclosed a portion of the very possible substance of negotiations. Each of them diminished, in other words, the dimensions of the possible *Verhandlungsgegenstand* [object of negotiation]. It was idle to suppose that a Germany which had once become a part of the EVG [European Defense Community] or of NATO would any longer be in a position to discuss freely with the Russians the question that most greatly interested them: namely, the question of the military future of Germany, and the nature of Germany's alliances. Each of these steps actually had the quality of a *fait accompli*, in the presence of which there was, for the Russians, just that much less to negotiate about. To ascertain *"ob es die Sowjetunion wirklich ernst meinte"* ["whether the Soviet Union was truly serious"] one would have had to hold these questions open and to talk with the Kremlin about them while one still had some freedom of action. To enter the EVG or NATO meant simply to decide them without negotiation; and in this case it would never be possible—and never was possible—to find out what the Russians would have been willing to pay for a solution more agreeable to them.[37]

On December 6, 1972, Bucerius persisted and repeated his question. In *Die Zeit* on April 20, 1984, Bucerius wrote "Aber von Kennan kein Rat" (But No Advice from Kennan), in which he quoted Kennan's response as reported by Countess Marion Dönhoff:

> Everyone, even the United States, wanted to include Germany in NATO (England and France feared Germany more than they feared Stalin). In other words, the policy was too well established and the coalition as such too inelastic. It would have taken too long for the three governments (and finally also the three high commissioners) to reach a new agreement.

> George Kennan believes that the Russians would certainly have paid a price to prevent Germany from joining NATO, and consequently he would have been in favor of finding out how high the

price would be. But, as stated, the coalition was too cumbersome and slow to allow this to occur.[38]

However, two sentences from Kennan's response are missing from *Die Zeit*. Kennan also stated: "The Americans have only attained something from the Russians when they have previously reached an understanding through secret negotiations." He added: "England and France were not averse to a divided Germany, nor did they mind a divided Europe, for, since the collapse of the Habsburg Empire, they have not developed a policy for Eastern Europe."

Even if Kennan had no advice to offer Bucerius in 1972–73, his thoughts about the exchange of notes in 1952 as ambassador to Moscow are nowhere so clearly stated as in his telegram from August 27, 1952.[39]

No one could expect the Soviets to lay all their cards on the table in a public exchange of notes. Much of what was in the note was unsatisfactory and stood in need of clarification—at the negotiating table. In contrast to Graml, Loth sees "proof of their seriousness precisely in the lack of attractiveness"[40] of the Soviet proposals. As the documents now make clear, this was exactly the opinion of the U.S. High Commission in Bonn. Moreover, a number of points permit various interpretations: "free elections in a unified Germany," "organizations opposed to peace and democracy," and the aspirations for a "peaceful, democratic, and independent" Germany were all ambiguous concepts. In Moscow and East Berlin, these terms had a different meaning than in the West. For the Communists, the elections in the Eastern bloc, which the West considered circumscribed, were the models for "free elections." Only Communist states were considered "peaceloving, democratic, and independent"; most of the non-Communist states were denounced as enemies of peace and democracy.

In the Eastern accompaniment to the note produced by the SED and its propagandists, these concepts reappeared. However, whether the note should be interpreted as a disruptive maneuver or even as a political and ideological offensive on the basis of Communist semantics is doubtful.[41] Clearly, certain statements were not inclined to make the note more attractive to the West Germans: as for example, when the SED spoke with enthusiastic approbation of a "world historic initiative" and of a program for the "national rebirth of Germany," or when Grotewohl, while interpreting the note in the Peoples' Chamber on March 14, described the GDR as the stronghold of democratic freedoms and the Federal Republic, by contrast, as the place of war criminals and anti-Semites, or when he characterized Adenauer's policy as anticonstitutional and thus pointed to the necessity of creating a truly peace-loving, democratic Germany on the model of the GDR.[42] And unsettling the West Germans was probably the intent of the SED leaders, who were apparently insecure about the Kremlin's new course.

Stalin's offer was not without risks for the Soviet Union. Sacrificing SED control could have led to unanticipated consequences throughout the entire Eastern bloc. Also, creating a national army, a nonmilitary economy, and trade without any barriers for a unified Germany would not necessarily have strengthened opposition to the European Defense Community among Western Europeans. This was especially true in France, where German soldiers were considered a nightmare, especially German soldiers in their own national uniform. Thus, Stalin's offer clearly persuaded the French that the European Defense Community was worth supporting and therefore enabled the negotiations to be quickly concluded. The Kremlin was apparently prepared to accept these risks: the stakes were high, but the price seemed worth it. Even if the presumption were true that Stalin's course within the Kremlin was not unchallenged, in March 1952 Stalin could have won. (Developments after his death in 1953 actually point to the existence of two schools of thought, as W. Loth observed: "One dogmatic, which gave preference to the 'construction of socialism' in the GDR, and one willing to take risks, which expected greater advantages for the Soviet Union from a neutralized Germany under certain conditions."[43])

Even the French Communists accepted the new course. Their behavior is further proof of the seriousness of the Soviet offer—proof that existing research has still scarcely explored. Although they had previously been passionately opposed to (West) German rearmament, not to mention to a national army, they began to come around to the new Soviet line. On March 14, the acting general secretary of the French Communist Party (PCF), Jacques Duclos, explained that a united Germany should be entitled to its own army for defensive purposes. For the American embassy in Paris, this "abrupt about-face" was clearly attributable to a wink from Moscow. Since this switch had been carried out with even greater discipline and speed than in 1939 after the signing of the Hitler–Stalin pact, the American embassy felt that it "merit[ed] vigorous treatment by VOA [Voice of America]."[44]

What is frequently lost sight of is that the first note and, with certain reservations, the second note were decisive for the entire exchange of notes in 1952. Graml's first conclusion—that firmly establishing the GDR as a member of the Soviet bloc could be facilitated by placing the blame at the West's door—applies only to the third Soviet note from

May 24, 1952, which was composed after the Soviet offer had been rejected and shortly before the treaties with the Western powers were signed, and not to the first and second notes as Graml implies. The U.S. High Commission in Bonn came to this same conclusion, in a summary analysis on June 2.[45] Only thus can the unmistakable gulf between the second and third notes be explained; only the third note became propaganda, as Kennan also clearly pointed out.[46] Only this third note adopted familiar Soviet positions. However, as the U.S. High Commission in Bonn noted, whatever the Kremlin leaders did, they carefully tried to create the impression of leaving the door to German talks open. The note was more than just the work of agitators.[47]

Considering all the evidence, there can no longer be any doubt that Stalin was prepared to agree to German reunification in the spring of 1952. The only question remains how far he was in fact prepared to go. For the West, "exploring the ramifications of the note" was considered possible and would not have endangered the treaties. This is an essential conclusion that can be drawn from the British and American documents.

CHAPTER TWO

THE FIRST SOVIET NOTE,
MARCH 10, 1952
Was Adenauer "More American
than the Americans"?

When the Stalin Note was presented, Adenauer "immediately and without hesitation smothered" all attempts to explore the ramifications of the note,[1] thereby seriously burdening his policy. Since then he has been accused of having bungled the last real chance for reunification, indeed, of having consciously rejected it. His decision contributed to a bitter discussion and to doubts that have left an immense scar on the history of the Federal Republic.

What considerations were motivating Adenauer in the spring of 1952 when he made his "epochal decision," as Theodor Schieder refers to it?[2] This decision can be understood only in the entire context of his foreign and domestic policy[3] and by keeping in mind how the situation appeared to him during those weeks.

Jacob Kaiser accused Adenauer of being "more American than the Americans" at a cabinet meeting; the phrase was repeated by McCloy, who did not specify which cabinet member held this view. See J. McCloy in Bonn to D. Acheson, March 28, 1952. DoS 662.001/3-2952.

The immediate reasons behind Adenauer's decision are well known and underlie his policy of uniting with the West:

1. His aspiration to avoid Germany's again seeking a separate path (the presumed or actual *Sonnderweg,* now historically repudiated), that is, to turn Germany's face toward the West once and for all.

2. His desire to free (West) Germany from its miserable vacillation between East and West.

3. His fear of a "super Versailles," his "Potsdam complex," that is, his fear of having something dictated by the victors, of having negotiations concerning Germany without equal participation by the Germans.

4. His concern about a revival of German nationalism, together with his pessimistic evaluation of the political capabilities of most Germans, including the leaders of the political parties.

5. His conviction "that the German people were not strong enough— neither politically, militarily, and physically nor mentally and temperamentally—to safeguard a free and independent central position in Europe between the giants in the East and West."[4]

Arnulf Baring pointed out a long time ago that, for Adenauer, the European Defense Community was an "end in itself, not a means to an end" and that reunification could not be "a substitute for Western European integration."[5] And in line with the concerns expressed above, the European Defense Community was indeed a goal, a Western European federation into which the Federal Republic could be "incorporated," so to speak. But was this the "final goal," did Adenauer have no further considerations? What remained of Adenauer's assertion that this "marching off of the Federal Republic into the West," as Gustav Heinemann called it at the time,[6] was also the shortest route to reunification? Were all of his professions favoring reunification just one gigantic lie? Did he fail to realize that integration into the Western alliance and reunification were mutually exclusive? Was he so naive— which I doubt—as to hope for Western solidarity on this issue and to believe Western pronouncements supporting reunification?

Without insinuating that Adenauer did not desire reunification at all, we cannot conclusively answer these questions. Does his greatness perhaps lie precisely in his relinquishing from the beginning any thought of reunification after prudently appraising all possible alternatives? Was the situation the way Arnulf Baring—who now views Adenauer more sympathetically—described it at the seventh "Aschaffenburg talks" on May 12, 1984?

Adenauer deceived his own people when he asserted that reunification was the highest goal of his policy. He even tricked them into believing that the Stalin Note of March 1952 proved that one could attain much more with patience and forbearance—a pure falsehood! But this was precisely Adenauer's greatness, that he was the first to perceive that no possibility existed for reunification in freedom and that the neutralization of a reunified Germany would signify political suicide.

At the "Aschaffenburg talks," protests against this view were inevitable. Rudolf Morsey argued passionately that such a lie about a central political issue would not be sustainable for decades.[7]

How did Adenauer argue at that time, and how should his arguments be evaluated? In the Bundestag debate on February 7, 1952, even before the Stalin Note, he stated: "I believe that we will attain Germany's reunification only with the help of the three Western allies, *never* with the help of the Soviet Union."[8] If he really believed that, how could reunification be realized? Did he mean, if not with the Soviet Union, then against it? In his response, Erich Ollenhauer asked Adenauer whether he was conscious of the considerable domestic and international significance of this assertion: "For if we do not believe in an open conflict between West and East . . . , then the proposition about achieving union with the help of the three Western powers is false." And further:"How does incorporating the Federal Republic into the defensive system of the West affect the question of German unity?"[9] These were, in fact, the central questions.

Adenauer gave his prescription at a CDU party congress in Heidelberg on March 1, 1952:

When the West is stronger than Soviet Russia, then the time to negotiate with Soviet Russia is at hand. Then, on the one hand, the fear of Germany will be removed. Then one will also need to explain to Soviet Russia that it is not acceptable, that it is impossible to keep half of Europe in slavery and that as a precondition to a settlement—not an armed conflict, but a peaceful settlement—circumstances in Eastern Europe must be reclarified.[10]

On March 5, in an interview with Ernst Friedländer, Adenauer emphasized this point: "Only when the West is strong enough will a genuine starting point exist for peaceful negotiations with the goal of liberating not only the Soviet zone but all the enslaved countries of Europe eastward of the iron curtain, and of liberating them in peace."[11]

And when the note lay on the table, he again referred precisely to this aspect. On March 16 at the first session of the Protestant Working Circle of the CDU in Siegen, he clearly defined his views on the Stalin Note for the first time, publicly and in principle:

> Let us be clear about one thing: there [in the East] sits the enemy of Christianity. We are dealing not only with political but with spiritual dangers. . . . Germany has three possibilities: alliance with the West, alliance with the East, and neutralization. However, neutralization means our declaring Germany a no-man's-land. With that, we would become an object and would no longer be a subject. Union with the East, however, is out of the question because our ideologies are so completely at variance. Union with the West—and I would like to say this to the East—in no way signifies any pressure on the East; it means nothing more than the preparation for a peaceful restructuring of relationships with respect to the Soviet Union, to German reunification, and to reorganization in Eastern Europe. And these are also political goals.

Then he turned directly to the note:

> It essentially offers little that is new. Apart from a strong nationalist touch, it advocates the neutralization of Germany and aims to impede progress in creating the European Defense Community and in integrating Europe.

He rejected the idea of national armed forces for Germany:

> Even to equip a few divisions would require enormous sums that we cannot even begin to think about, and therefore this provision in the Soviet note is nothing more than paper, simply paper! But the note exists and it must be responded to, and it does indicate a certain progress, even though to a much lesser degree than is generally believed. Therefore, we must not overlook any possibility of coming to a peaceful understanding and to a reorganization in the sense I described. On the other hand, we cannot under any circumstances permit a delay to hamper the creation of the European Defense Community, for such a delay would probably also mean the end of these joint efforts. . . . If these matters are not concluded now, then in my view the opportunities will be lost forever. Therefore I repeat: our general position with regard to the note must be that we cannot fail to fully explore every possibility of quickly attaining a reorganization of Eastern Europe. However, even less can we stop a project

that is nearing completion, for then matters would become very grave. . . . We want the West to be so strong that it can conduct reasonable talks with the Soviet government, and I am firmly convinced that this last note from Soviet Russia validates this position. When we continue as we have been, when the West, including the United States, is as strong as it must be, when it is stronger than the Soviet government, then is the time when the Soviet government will listen. The goal of a dialogue between West and East, however, will be to safeguard the peace in Europe, to halt the meaningless arms race, to reunify Germany in peace, and to restructure the East. Then, finally, the world will attain what it has urgently needed during all the previous decades: a long and secure peace! [12]

When speaking to the executive committee of CDU Bundestag members, Adenauer persisted in asserting that reunification must be seen in connection with a solution to the entire issue of Eastern Europe:

When the reorganization of Europe comes—and it will come—then one will not be able to overlook a reorganization in Eastern Europe, even in the satellite states. . . . When these talks come, they cannot be restricted to the Soviet zone of Germany but must involve all of Eastern Europe. For this reason, these talks with the Soviets should not occur too early, since matters are not yet far enough along. We must speak to the Soviets at the proper moment. This will only be possible when the West is strong, so that the Soviets will listen to us and to the West. I have great confidence that the Soviets do not want to fight a war. And when will these decisive talks take place? In any case, we will not need to wait many years. With General Eisenhower as president of the United States, all this will proceed more rapidly because this conforms to his own conception. Consequently, we must accept that our nerves will be greatly strained in the short run. Negotiating with the Soviets at this stage would be downright harmful for us. [13]

A Western course would thus bring about not only reunification but also the liberation of Eastern Europe. Did Adenauer seriously believe this, or was he only interested, as Arnulf Baring believed, in "shaming those who now pressed for negotiations and telling them to wait a little while longer, and then something completely different would be possible, namely the reorganization of Eastern Europe"? [14] This was probably also part, but not all, of the truth; otherwise, how can his comments from March 1 and 5 be explained? Why did he argue in the same fashion in his *Erinnerungen* (Memoirs)?

> Only when the West was strong would there be a genuine starting point for peace negotiations, with the goal of liberating not only the Soviet zone but all of enslaved Europe eastward of the iron curtain, and doing so in peace. Following the path to the European Defense Community seemed to me the best service we could render the Germans in the Soviet zone.[15]

What deliberations influenced Adenauer's assessment of Soviet policy? In his *Erinnerungen*, he answers this question thoroughly:

> The Soviet Union had undertaken too many tasks. It could not simultaneously build up its empire . . . into a well-functioning state, do justice to its enormous domestic tasks, and also keep pace with the United States in the arms race. It could not do all these things for the simple reason that its agricultural base was not sufficient to feed its population because of a lack of arable land and a shortage of workers and machines. Soviet Russia could not wear down the West; it could also not continue to live with the West in the current climate of tension, particularly with the Chinese lurking dangerously in the background. Developments would one day force a choice: either conflict with, and conquest of, Western Europe or conflict with the Chinese.[16] Soviet Russia was anxious to create a communist Asia according to Soviet conceptions. Conflict with the Chinese was inevitable, since the Chinese were also attempting to bolshevize Asia, but according to Chinese conceptions and under Asian leadership. My hope was that the Soviet would one day realize that they could not do everything. I also hoped they would then focus on their conflicts with the Chinese and leave Europe alone. We must wait for their decision. In order for developments to take this course, the free countries of Western Europe must be united; France, as one of the pivotal countries, must certainly play a decisive role in this union. A European alliance was needed to make Soviet Russia realize that Europe was so closely unified that nothing more could be broken off, that nothing more could be done there. And to simultaneously go after a unified Europe, the United States, and China would be impossible. We must patiently await this recognition.[17]

Adenauer regularly invited selected journalists to confidential discussions. The records of these "tea talks" provide a further source,[18] one that is certainly not as elevated as the historian might wish, but one that nonetheless provides a clue to the chancellor's concerns and, especially, to his means of shaping public opinion to conform with his way of thinking. Some ideas appear and reappear in these records, almost to excess. For example, the Soviet Union's goal was to isolate Germany through neutralization, in order to make European integration impossible and, finally, in the course of the cold war, to conquer all of Europe. France and Italy were not strong enough to bring about European integration; Great Britain had its own interests; and, in such circumstances, the United States would withdraw from Europe in disappointment (Europe would "become Russian; that is not too weakly formulated, it must be seen for what it is").[19] "All this would be the continuation of a drama, whose first act was the subjugation of the satellite states begun in 1945."[20] The isolation and neutralization of Germany would mean "that Germany, stuck between the two strong power blocs, would finally be pulled into the Russian maelstrom."[21] Neutralization would be equivalent to Germany's "suicide"[22]; it would "bring free Germany into slavery together with the Eastern zone."[23]

Thus the question of restoring unity was not the decisive issue for Adenauer, but "*one* of a very large bundle of issues,"[24] part of "a number of issues almost encompassing the earth."[25] When the Soviet Union was one day ready to negotiate—"and that day will come, I am convinced"[26]—then the negotiations would not concern only the Soviet zone; "then this issue will no longer play a role," then the concern will be "appeasing the entire Eastern European territory and most probably also the East Asian territory."[27] Liberation of the Soviet zone would lead to a movement for freedom in the satellite states, beginning in Poland. Poland would then be "the westernmost pillar against the Eastern oppression."[28] The prerequisites for beginning such negotiations would be the West's strength and the Soviet Union's understanding that Europe could no longer be conquered, because of Western consolidation. Adenauer never tired of referring to the Soviet Union's "significant domestic problems," especially to its problems with agriculture, and to the necessity of solving them ("even a dictatorship with Asian characteristics needs to feed its people"). In his view, the Soviets would more willingly turn their attention to these problems once they understood that there was nothing more to be done in Europe.[29]

Even Hillgruber has referred to Adenauer's failure in 1952 to make a prudent and realistic assessment of the Soviet Union's power in the world—and especially its German policy. When Adenauer simultaneously warned about the danger in the East and hoped to force the Soviet Union into a defensive posture, this reflected the "well-known, peculiarly double-sided 'image' of Russia that was popular for decades in Germany and throughout Western Europe, in which an overestimation of the Soviet Union's threat to Europe was coupled with the expectation of a sudden collapse of the Soviet empire as a result of its overexertion. Fear and illusory hope were all tangled up together."[30]

For Adenauer, the European Defense Community, with its planned European political union, was "far and away the most important historical event for Europe in hundreds of years."[31] In this sense, the European Defense Community was "the goal of his policy," while also serving as the "means to the goal" of engaging the Soviet Union in an almost global conflict. But the European Defense Community could not in any way be considered an object for barter when dealing with Stalin over reunification. Here, two mutually exclusive principles collided with one another. "No offer from the Soviet Union" could move him, Adenauer emphasized on June 2, 1952, "to break off ties to the West."[32] Such a break in relations would involve surrendering the Federal Republic "finally to the Asian East."

For Adenauer, reunification was "not a goal in and of itself, but only a link in a long chain of conflicts between East and West."[33] The Germany proposed by the Russian dictator—unaligned, but armed—had no place in Adenauer's thinking, and it would not have found a place, even if Stalin had improved his offer. For Adenauer, there was nothing to be negotiated concerning such a German. Thus, for him, there was nothing in the note requiring clarification; the note did not constitute an opportunity and thus could be immediately rejected on principle. Having virtually achieved his goal of signing the treaties with the West, Adenauer would not let anything mar his success, which had been difficult enough to attain. His entire strength and all his abilities were involved in achieving three goals: blocking negotiations with the Soviet Union, completing the treaties with the West as quickly as possible and, presenting these moves to his own party and to the German people as the only correct and, at the same time, the shortest path to reunification. Great efforts to convince people were not required, however; many already believed as he did.

In the cabinet, only the minister for all-German affairs, Jakob Kaiser, opposed him. In the cabinet meeting on the morning of March 11, a "rather bitter dispute" broke out between Kaiser and Adenauer. Kaiser emphasized that one "must take a positive attitude in any case," even if the note was directed at the Western powers. Adenauer was of another opinion: the note was directed "first to France, in an attempt to bring the French back around to their old, traditional policy toward

Russia. One should not under any circumstances awaken the suspicion that we are vacillating in our policy." Kaiser believed "that a national German Army would be more valuable than a European army! Adenauer stressed that the European states alone were not in a position to defend themselves." Dehler supported Adenauer and affirmed that only brutal candor would help. This was also the view of Minister of the Interior Robert Lehr, whereas Heinrich Hellwege pointed out that, according to this note, the Soviets must believe that Germany should renounce German territory in the East.[34]

On the afternoon of March 11, Adenauer reported his decision in principle to the high commissioners. According to the British short protocol, the decisive part of the meeting went as follows: First, the chairman, André François-Poncet, explained that the Russians proposed a conference whenever they wanted to put a stop to what they considered an unpleasant development. He felt that the Western powers and the Federal Republic needed to retain their basic demand, that free elections throughout a unified Germany would constitute the first step toward reunification and toward the conclusion of a peace treaty, for to do so would provide a good way of measuring the Russians goodwill. According to the protocol, it was then *Adenauer* who declared that the Russian note would change nothing in his government's policy. The cabinet had debated the note in the morning and had agreed on a certain statement for the press, since, for the uninformed reader, the note contained some deceptive elements. The Soviets' goal was to neutralize Germany, a goal made more palatable by allowing for a national army. However, the Federal Republic did not want a national army; moreover, Germany was not at all in a position to equip its own modern army. The other remarkable aspect of the note was the way it flattered the Nazis and the German militarists.

Adenauer did not actually know whether the note was directed more to the French parliament or to the German parties of the right. He proposed, and also hoped, that the three Western powers would quickly respond to the note, since otherwise the German public would be seriously alarmed. He thus assumed that the Western powers would not agree to a four-power conference. U.S. High Commissioner John McCloy emphasized that the Soviet note provided the best proof of the success of previous integration policy, and his British colleague Ivone Kirkpatrick added that if one were to successfully pursue negotiations concerning integration, the Soviets would sooner or later make a better offer. Adenauer agreed.[35]

Adenauer's *Erinnerungen*, reads differently. Whereas he usually reproduced his talks with the high commissioners completely accurately in his memoirs, he probably had good reason to curtly summarize this discussion in the following sentence: "I therefore greatly welcome the three Western powers' affirmation through their high commissioners immediately following their receipt of the Russian note on March 11: 'We will continue our negotiations concerning the European Defense Community and the Bonn Convention just as though the note did not exist!' "[36]

Wilhelm Grewe, a participant in the discussion with the high commissioners, recognized the discrepancy between fact and fiction when he pointed to this sentence in his *Rückblenden* (Flashbacks) and emphasized that Adenauer had "misconstrued" the statements of the high commissioners.[37] A significant misunderstanding!

A critical element at that time was the Western powers' knowledge that Adenauer would not budge. Thus, there was no need for talks with the Soviets. The question of how the West should have reacted if Adenauer, the opposition, and public opinion had demanded an examination of the Soviet offer and of the possible reunification of Germany in accordance with the terms of this offer—thus a militarily unaligned Germany—remained hypothetical from the beginning and thus was never discussed at all. At least, the available documents do not refer to any such discussion.

With Adenauer on the side of the Western powers, with his immediate and decisive rejection of any attempts to explore or probe the note, the statements of CDU politicians with other views on the matter lost their significance. In a radio broadcast on March 12, Kaiser spoke out against "all too hasty expressions of opinion," by which he apparently meant the Federal Press Secretary Felix von Eckardt's statement from the previous day:

> No one can deny that the Soviet Union's proposals for a peace treaty with Germany constitute one of the important political events of the past few months. This should also be recognized through cautious reserve with respect to the content and intention of the note. Germany and the Western powers will certainly need to verify carefully whether a turning point in the relations between East and West has been reached.[38]

As a result, a renewed disagreement between Kaiser and Adenauer broke out in the cabinet meeting on March 14. According to Hans-Peter Schwarz, who relies on the diary of Otto Lenz, then undersecretary in the chancellor's office, Adenauer asserted:

The treaties are essentially negotiated. The Russian note is chiefly a disruptive attempt to exploit the weaknesses of the French government. Our foremost duty now is to keep quiet. Kaiser defends himself by stating that he had to speak out because the statements made by the press and the information office were inadequate. Even McCloy and François-Poncet agree. Ultimately one must remember that everything could become completely different. One could not now be quiet but would need to speak. Adenauer stubbornly insists on his viewpoint: the cabinet unanimously decided that the government should not take a position. Therefore Kaiser's taking a position is out of the question. Significantly, [Kaiser] was questioned by the high commissioners, which leads one to presume that they were not in complete agreement with Kaiser's speech. In his view, the Federal Republic should have quietly let the others speak first. For the allies it would certainly have been very convenient if the Germans had spoken first. Kaiser then relents and remarks that now he, too, only wants to support the chancellor's policy. One must drag the Western allies, who are not united among themselves, along as well.[39]

Four days later, Kaiser declared, again on the radio, that abroad some perhaps believed (and in this he was correct) that the division of Germany was not the worst of the postwar decisions and that the Federal Republic should "thus help clarify the German question by making a proposal of its own." However, because of the situation, this could only be a Germany reduced in size by the loss of the territory east of the Oder and Neisse rivers and unaligned, just as "a Switzerland made enormously larger would be averse to a commitment to any one side," as Paul Sethe put it on March 22 in the *Frankfurter Allgemeine Zeitung*.

However, support for such a Germany found no majority, neither in the government nor in the coalition! Those who sympathized with Sethe were in a hopeless minority; no one had the stature to gather together the "dispersed skeptics," as Arnulf Baring called them, and then to risk a possible rebellion; all the prerequisites for this were lacking. In the CDU/CSU, there was only a "feeble and unfocused all-German protest."[40] The Protestants in the CDU/CSU supported Adenauer's policy after his talk in Siegen and described "any form" of neutralization as "impossible"; integration into the West would not deepen the division of Germany. The council of the Protestant Church in Germany, Catholic organizations, and a large part of the press reacted similarly.[41] By reading the views being expressed at the time, we can clearly see the entrenched attitudes that Stalin's offer encountered. At the Bundestag session on April 3, Kurt Georg Kiesinger deemed Adenauer's view "completely correct." Russia, he argued, "has much more to offer us and the West than it has offered to date. Only if we continue negotiations and come to an understanding with the West will Soviet Russia be forced (Representative Renner: "Aha! Forced!") to make true proposals."[42]

Martin Euler, FDP party leader, was convinced that "in the meantime, the course of the cold war has changed: the offensive position has shifted to include the entire Western world." Hans Joachim von Merkatz of the German Party demanded the "acceleration of the process of withdrawal" of the Soviets' western boundary: "Russia is required to retreat one day, for its present position is simply not sustainable."[43] Undersecretary Walter Hallstein, who was in Washington when the note was delivered, spoke of reorganizing Europe up to the Ural Mountains. The press service of the CDU immediately greeted this with these words:

> This is certainly such an extensive goal that there is nothing left to be desired! Stages on the way to attaining this goal are naturally the integration of Western Europe, the peaceful reunification of Germany, the union of free European states, and finally unification with an Eastern Europe freed from Bolshevik tyranny. The goal is fixed and so are the means to it, for, with the currently existing relationships, the only path that can lead to this goal is this: the unrelenting buildup of the defensive strength of the free nations in order to attain a level of strength that will doom any Bolshevik aggression to failure from the start and thus, in the end, will force the expansionist drive of bolshevism into a decline.[44]

CHAPTER THREE

THE WESTERN POWERS: CONTROL OF THE FEDERAL REPUBLIC THROUGH INTEGRATION

What impressions, goals, and considerations motivated the Western powers in March of 1952? Did the Soviet offer perhaps come too late? Hans-Peter Schwarz conjectured that the Soviets "made a decisive error in their policy toward Germany" at the conference of deputy foreign minister held from March 5 to June 21, 1951, in the Palais Marbre Rose in Paris: "If Moscow had agreed without hesitation to a foreign ministers' conference and had taken that opportunity to present the proposals for neutralization that they later presented on March 10, 1952, in the form of the celebrated Stalin Note, future developments would have been completely unpredictable." The reason was that in the spring of 1951, "no decisions had yet been made concerning whether and in what form a German defense contribution would exist, nor what the future of the occupation regime should be."[1]

Is this argument really sound? In the spring of 1951, the Western allies, especially the Americans and the British, could hardly imagine not including a German defense contribution in their plans. And if a Soviet offer had been made, reaction to it would in no way have been unpredictable. On the contrary, in the secret game plans of the Western powers—for example, of the British—exactly the same suggestion that the Soviet Union made in 1952 had appeared in the summer of 1951. The answer was unambiguous: reunification under these conditions carried too many risks with it; the division of the country was always preferable.[2] In addition, representatives of other Western governments were also convinced that division was "a very good thing." For example, the Italian Chargé d'Affaires to London, during his first visit to the Foreign Office in January 1952—following several years of service in Moscow—expressed this opinion and added that he hoped division would persist for some time. The response of Frank Roberts, deputy undersecretary of state and head of the German section in the Foreign Office, was guarded: "German division undoubtedly helped towards her integration into Western Europe."[3]

In the event of an aggressive Soviet Union, what would happen to a Germany divided at the Elbe? This question had haunted the British chiefs of staff since the summer of 1944, but at that time, they encountered the opposition of career diplomats in the Foreign Office. In the spring of 1946, in view of Soviet policy, these diplomats seized upon these concerns and began purposefully pursuing responses to them. They succeeded in bringing the hesitant Americans around to their point of view in 1946–47.[4] Thus united, in the spring of 1948 they went ahead to establish the Federal Republic. The French tried to delay things to the best of their ability. One of their attempts at the beginning of May 1948 led to revealing comments concerning German unity by R. M. A. Hankey, the head of the northern department in the Foreign Office, who was also responsible for the Soviet Union. In his opinion, a united Germany represented a much greater danger to peace than did a divided Germany. He gave the following reasons:

> a. A united Germany is bound to be regarded as a real menace by Russia. She must always fear that it will be controlled by hostile powers and in her eyes any non-Communist power *is* hostile. Therefore she must inevitably try to control or ally herself with Germany.
> b. If Russia controls, or directs, or is allied with the whole of Germany, she will always be tempted to encourage Germany to expand westwards in order to keep German eyes away from the East. The combination of Russia and Germany would be an almost irre-

sistible menace to the Western world. We should therefore have infinitely more trouble with Russia than we do now.

c. A united Germany of 62 million or more *cannot* in my opinion be adequately controlled or directed by any methods the Western Powers can use, as we saw between the wars. Only the Russians can direct a united Germany through the Communist Party and Secret Police system.

d. A united non-Communist Germany allied to the Western Powers will, I suggest, start trouble at the earliest opportunity to regain their lost territories in the East. The Western Powers could not allow such a Germany to be destroyed and occupied by Russia. As an ally a united Germany would therefore be a most dangerous asset.

e. A united non-Communist Germany, even allied to the West, will, in my opinion, always be tempted to blackmail us by threatening to join Russia and, if [Point c] is correct, we could not be sure of preventing this.

f. A Western Germany of 40 million inhabitants all afraid of Russian aggression and penetration will depend on cooperation with the Western Powers for protection (it will obviously have to be armed by the way),[5] and will depend completely on the Western Powers for raw materials, food and markets; it will be less liable to invade Eastern Germany than a united Germany would be to invade Poland: In short, it would be far more amenable and far less of a danger to France.

g. In any case there obviously cannot be a united Germany. Neither we nor the Russians can allow the other to control Germany and it is plain, after the experience of the last three years, that we cannot agree to control Germany jointly. Given Russia's ideology, this has seemed inevitable for a long time, but obviously we had to try the experiment.[6]

This analysis met with approval in the Foreign Office. And nothing changed at all when, in July, under the direct effect of a total Berlin blockade, the British military governor in Germany, Brian Robertson, put forth a plan proposing to restore German unity: free elections in Germany, the formation of a central government in Berlin, and the withdrawal of the occupying troops in certain border areas. For their agreement, the Soviets were to be offered a role in controlling the Ruhr industries.

The Robertson Plan was intensively debated in the Foreign Office at the time and was finally rejected as too dangerous. The deputy under-secretary of state, Roger Makins, head of the economics section, voiced his objections:

> We must not underrate the extent to which the adoption of General Robertson's proposals would involve a complete overturn of our economic policy in Western Europe. Once we open negotiations on the basis proposed, we must not delude ourselves into thinking that we could draw a line at any particular point. The Russians would have the advantage at every turn, since having forced us into negoti-ations on unequal terms, their prestige and attractive power would be greatly increased; they would be able to put the screw on Berlin at any time; and we should be negotiating under a threat, however well it might be disguised.
>
> The disintegration of our policy would indeed be such that we could not expect to reconstitute it on any given line. We should be running into an economic "Munich" of major proportions.
>
> The plain fact is that we have gone too far with the Western European policy to reverse engines without grave damage to our interests, and the strong attitude of the Russians is a measure of their realization that we have gone so far and been successful. . . . In a word, if we embark on the Robertson Plan, it is the end of the Marshall Plan.[7]

Given the disadvantages, even the head of the German section in the Foreign Office, Patrick Dean, was swayed. The idea of having Russians in the Ruhr territory was intolerable to him. In addition, in his view, a central government in Berlin would inevitably fall under Soviet con-trol:

> I have always been the more nervous about this [the future control of the Ruhr] because of the extreme anxiety of the Russians to get into the Ruhr; and I have always felt, and feel more strongly than ever now, perhaps wrongly, that once the Russians got in, on how-ever small and respectable a basis, their influence would grow and grow and any chance of the Ruhr becoming in future years a con-tented and peaceful part of Western European economic activity would disappear.[8]

Christopher Steel, the head of the political section of the military government in Berlin, passionately denied this assertion:

> I believe the Germans to be more definitely anti-Communist than any people in Europe except the British and that in the long run we

are bound to have to build on them if the Communist flood is to be resisted. . . . By withdrawing our forces to the Rhine and merely covering the Ruhr from the west bank, as I should like to do, we shall be in no weaker position politically or militarily than we are now. . . . Neither do I think that the Russians in the Ruhr control machinery would be able to do much more for communism in the area than they do at present through their various underground means and they might well do the Communist cause active harm.

Steel, who was later to become ambassador to the Federal Republic, was concerned about *all* of Germany:

Of course I am assuming in all this that we should be actively pursuing a policy designed to bring Germany wholeheartedly into the western fold on a basis of ultimate equality. Once you have decided to have a single Germany between ourselves and the Russians and you have made up your mind that the Russians are permanently hostile, there is no other course open.[9]

Robertson could not persuade his critics. He and the other members of the military government found their sole supporter in Undersecretary Ivone Kirkpatrick, who was later to become the high commissioner in the Federal Republic. It was also Kirkpatrick who noted the lack of a clear alternative in any of the criticism of the Robertson Plan. Naturally, he also saw the risks inherent in this plan: no establishment of a Western-oriented state; participation of the Soviets in the control of the Ruhr territory; and a united Germany, either communist or nationalist, that might possibly slip away from Western control. But as Kirkpatrick concluded at the beginning of September 1948:

But as against this risk, we should be inviting the Russians to take the greater risk of loosening their hold on Eastern Germany and thus diminishing pro tanto the extent of the Russian Empire in Europe and its influence. . . . To sum up, I am disposed to agree with General Robertson that the least dangerous and therefore most attractive course is to plump for German unity with all its attendant risks.[10]

Independent of Robertson, the Policy Planning Staff at the U.S. State Department under George F. Kennan developed a similar plan. Among other things, this plan called for the withdrawal of the occupying troops and the reestablishment of an independent, all-German state: "We could then withdraw from Berlin without loss of prestige, and the people of the western sectors would not be subjected to Soviet rule because the Russians would also be leaving the city."[11]

The disadvantages that the Policy Planning Staff listed were similar to the objections that the Foreign Office raised against the Robertson Plan. Nevertheless, Robertson prevailed because the alternatives seemed even less tolerable and involved endless worry about the Berlin problem; about a West Germany that, without ties to the East and without the European federation that evidently had not got off the ground, would not be economically viable; about the Germans who were longing for reunification; and about the military security of Western Europe.

Both plans were superseded. On the one hand, the Kremlin was not prepared—because of Berlin and also because of the establishment of a Western-oriented state—to risk a war in which the West would need to resort to atomic weapons because it was conventionally inferior. On the other hand, the West Germans accepted the Western allies' plans for forming a Western state. "The Western Germans as a whole have cast away their doubts to such an extent, that there is a real chance that we shall get a Western German Government established and reasonably flourishing fairly soon," as Patrick Dean, head of the German section in the Foreign Office, commented on September 2, 1948.[12] In London and Washington, there was also the fear that in Western Europe, and especially in West Germany, a retreat would lead to a loss of confidence that would be hard to recoup. President Harry Truman also worried that people in the United States would attribute a retreat to weakness and that this would thus considerably damage his chances in the fall presidential elections. With the increasing success of the airlift, with the West Germans on the side of the Western powers, and with the certainty that the Soviets would not begin a war, those critics who from the outset had been opposed to a new beginning for German policy were proved correct. Since the autumn of 1948, the Americans and the British had had no further need to compromise with the Soviet Union. In September 1948, American Secretary of State George Marshall put it as follows:

> In every field the Russians are retreating. From now on, Berlin is the only foothold which they have against us: everywhere else, and particularly in Germany, they are losing ground. We have put Western Germany on its feet and we are engaged in bringing about its recovery in such a way that we can really say that we are on the road to victory.[13]

What would happen to (West) Germany in the long run was earnestly debated in Western capitals at that time. One of the most interesting documents originated in the British Foreign Office in November 1948; it comes from Undersecretary of State Kirkpatrick. For him, the entire German problem could be reduced to the theme of future safety from Germany. This was a reappearance of the Rappallo complex: Germany alone was no longer a danger; only as an ally of the Soviets would it become a "mortal peril." The first and, indeed, the only aim "must be to prevent her joining the Soviet bloc." To attain this goal, one should not run after the Germans, the "best chisellers" in Europe, telling them how important they were or they would play the West off against the East.

Kirkpatrick also objected to ongoing control of West Germany through the three Western powers with the assistance of the Military Security Board. This might perhaps be the best solution if one were sure the Germans could not at any time play the Russian card. He vigorously argued for throwing the old "Security Shibboleths" overboard and for attaining security from Germany by integrating Germany, that is, including it in the "Western Union club"—but at a time when this could be sold to the Germans as a "favour" and not the other way around. The logic was clear: it was a matter of "bamboozling the Germans by roping them in" and "eventually making them so dependent economically, politically and militarily on the Western world that they cannot afford to break away and joint the East." In this way, the West should be able to keep a tight grip on the development of the German economy and German policy; at a later stage, rearmament—with full military dependence on the Western armies—could even be considered. Under the "cloak of equal rights" for West Germany, the West would attain complete control through more effective means than making the (proposed) Military Security Board a permanent institution.[14]

Foreign Minister Ernest Bevin described Kirkpatrick's observations as a "thoughtful contribution"; in essence, they anticipated the actual course of events. Seventeen months later, on April 26, 1950, Bevin asserted in a secret cabinet paper that the West should pursue a policy of "gradually bringing the Federal Republic into closer association with the West" by accepting them into international organizations. To those critics who argued that by following this policy the West would make more final the division of Germany, he replied that he did not think these fears were well founded since "the division of Germany is an accomplished fact."[15]

At more or less the same time, Sir William Strang, permanent undersecretary of state and thus the highest official in the Foreign Office, presented a strategy paper dealing with the problem of the "unity or division of Germany."[16] Under Strang's leadership, experts in the Foreign Office began working on this "top secret" study in the autumn of 1949 and completed it on April 19, 1950. Even though only a few possibilities were explored and American and French interests were not taken into account at all, so that it was impossible to immediately translate anything into practical policy, this study is highly interesting. It clearly shows how the subject of "unity or division" was discussed in the straightforward and unemotional terms of realpolitik. Although the balance came down heavily on the side of permanent division, this document presents possibilities and alternatives. It also shows that many public proclamations made later in connection with Western reunification efforts had already been identified as propaganda, and that an agreement with the Soviet Union concerning Germany was ruled out from the beginning in case NATO membership should be offered to a united Germany—a position that was publicly given an entirely different interpretation two years later during the exchange of diplomatic notes with the Soviet Union. Another interesting aspect is the assumption that Germany would continue to remain demilitarized, since this assumption contrasts with the course of events later that same year: in August 1950, Adenauer proposed a German military contribution, and shortly thereafter, the Western powers decided in principle to rearm West Germany.

In the opinion of this working group in the Foreign Office, the permanent division of Germany carried with it a number of disadvantages and dangers for the West:

1. The fact that no four-power accord existed was primarily an indication of the worldwide struggle between communism and "Western" civilization, but this lack of an agreement had itself become one of the major factors in the tension between East and West.

2. In a divided Germany without a peace treaty, the appeal to unity could be used to inflame German nationalism.

3. In the contest between the great powers, Germany had become a pawn that both sides wished to turn into a queen on the political chessboard. This might also be the case with a democratic central government, but the fact remained that, as long as four-power control did not exist, it would be easier for the Germans to blackmail the Western powers and the Soviet Union in turn and "so to recover their strength as a nation and a dominant influence in Europe."

4. The position of the Western powers in Berlin remained precarious in a divided Germany.

5. The longer the Russians maintained their grip on the Eastern zone, the harder it would be ever to bring that zone within the Federal Republic.

In view of these factors, both the Western powers and the Soviet Union were faced with the question of what best served their long-term interests: the permanent division or the reunification of Germany. Two alternatives existed for the Soviets: reunification following negotiations with the Western powers or the conversion of East Germany into a fully equipped satellite. For the Western powers, the fundamental questions were which of these alternatives would be more advantageous to the West and what Western policy should be in each case.

From a Western viewpoint, what conditions would need to be fulfilled to make an agreement with the Soviets possible? A reunified Germany (1) free of foreign domination, (2) independent of external economic help, and (3) incapable of renewed aggression. Additional demands included:

a. free elections
b. the right to join certain international organizations such as the Council of Europe and the Organization for European Economic Cooperation
c. an occupation statute—or something similar—for the four powers without the right of veto
d. basic liberties
e. four-power agreement on certain economic issues (currency, reparations, and prohibited and limited industries)
f. participation by all of Germany's former adversaries in drafting a peace treaty
g. guarantees by both the allied signatories and the German government concerning Germany's borders
h. permission for Germany to form a gendarmerie
i. complete prohibition of the armaments industry
j. final settlement of reparations
k. dissolution of the *Sovietaktiengesellschaften*[17]

What could induce the Soviets to negotiate with the West?
1. They could be swayed by any loss of their influence in the Western sectors.
2. They might expect that, following an agreement, American troops would withdraw from Europe, whereas their own would only withdraw to Poland, and that in the long run the United States' interest in

defending Europe would subside. Germany, even reunified, would be no match for Russia in a modern war. Therefore, if Russia were looking around for allies, it could hope to win all of Germany for itself by pointing to the weakness of Western Europe—especially if American support were in decline—and by alluding to the traditional German belief in the shared interests of the Slavic and Teutonic peoples. To attain this goal, Russia only needed to appeal to German nationalism, not to first convert Germany to communism.

3. Continuing to allow SED puppets to govern the Soviet sector could prove embarrassing. In the long run, creating an East German government could weaken Russian control over the East German population.

4. Reunification could therefore prove attractive by enabling the Communists to improve their image throughout Germany and at least attain a position such as that held by the Communists in Italy. Even with little chance of coming to power, they could continue to play an important role as a strong minority party and win concessions from the government. Even if all of Germany could not be transformed into a Russian satellite, the Russians could at least still hope to make Germany into a buffer state between East and West.

5. At the same time, the Russians would no longer need to grant concessions to East Germany and make promises to West Germany to outdo the Western powers in their German policy. They might possibly even hope to persuade the Western powers to support a more repressive policy in Germany. In addition, Russia would become a member of the Military Security Board and possibly even of the International Ruhr Authority.

6. As a result of reunification, the standard of living in East Germany would be brought into line with that in West Germany; thus the Russians could rid themselves of the burden of being solely responsible for an area in need of emergency assistance.

What advantages did a united Germany offer the West?

1. Because of the existing tensions and conflicts between the two German states, the permanent division of Germany could contribute to incidents [of hostility]. A second Berlin blockade would pose a greater danger for peace than did the first in 1948–49.

2. Under a central government, the Russians would have to relinquish control of the Eastern sector. And as their control lessened, so would their influence in Europe.

3. The Western powers had the chance, especially during the Mar-

shall Plan, to bring all of Germany under Western influence. It might also be possible to reduce Russian influence in Eastern Europe.

4. When formulating policy toward Germany, the Western powers needed increasingly to consider the desires of the Germans, just as the Russians were having to do. In addition, the Russians could entice the West Germans with "German unity" at any time. An agreement with the Soviets would put an end to this Russian tactic.

5. German exports could be steered toward markets where they would no longer present such competition for the British economy.

What disadvantages did a united Germany pose for the West?

1. Russian troops in Poland would probably be no less dangerous than Russian troops at the Elbe.

2. Reunification would enhance the efficiency and the competitive capabilities of the German economy and would damage the economies of the other Western European nations. As a member of the International Ruhr Authority, the Russians might possibly attempt to divert Germany's industrial resources toward Eastern Europe in return for raw materials. In this way, Russia would indirectly profit from the Marshall Plan and thereby weaken Western Europe.

3. The Russians might attempt to build up all of Germany as a base of expansion to the West.

4. As an alternative, the Russians might try to join with the Western powers to neutralize Germany and to make it into a buffer state between East and West in the hope of later winning it for themselves.

5. No democratic tradition existed in Germany. Despite two defeats, the German people probably still identified with Friedrich Nietzche's "superman" and Adolf Hitler's "master race," with the result that the Germans might attempt to regain "former German territory," such as Austria, the Saar, the Sudetenland, East Prussia, and the "Polish 'recovered territories'" east of the Oder–Neisse frontier, and thus to reestablish a central European power 90 million people strong.

6. Reunification would mean the end of military occupation and the withdrawal of American troops from Europe, with all the inevitable effects on European confidence and security. It would probably not be possible to prevent Germany from embarking on any political experiment, however undesirable.

In conclusion, the risks of coming to an agreement with the Soviets on reunification were described as "very real"; nevertheless, it was acknowledged that the only way of achieving reunification was through negotiations with the Soviets. If the Soviets were to (1) make no offer, (2) make an offer that was unacceptable to the West, or (3) disrupt negotiations, then the West's alternative was a policy that had to be based on the continued division of Germany. Publicly, one could continue to support reunification or, at a suitable moment for propaganda purposes, to propose all-German elections and the formation of a constituent assembly under terms that the Russians "in their present mood could not accept." As long as there was no satisfactory Soviet proposal for reunification, "the Western powers can only continue their present policy of associating Western Germany more closely with the consolidated Western world."

In reading this document, the question arises: What would have happened if the premises on which the British planners based their conclusions had been fulfilled, that is, if rearmament had not taken place? Adenauer's proposal for a German military contribution fundamentally altered the prerequisites. Interestingly enough, even after the decision in principle favoring rearmament was made in the autumn of 1950 as a result of massive American pressure, William Strang remained a determined opponent of this policy, and in December 1950, vehement discussions took place in the Foreign Office.

Strang's study met with considerable criticism even in his own ranks. Sir Brian Robertson, high commissioner in the Federal Republic since August 1949, completely rejected the study on May 5, 1950, and adopted a diametrically opposed position. He did so in part because the question of union or division was not clearly answered, and in part because he had been convinced since the autumn of 1949 that the West could be defended only with the help of German troops. In his view, the West could not remain on the defensive in the issue of reunification and leave the field to the Soviets; on the contrary, the West must assume the offensive and propose reunification "today, tomorrow and the next day," but under conditions that implied Germany's integration into the West and were "totally unacceptable to the Soviet and [would] remain so until she realize[d] that her game [was] up."[18]

A week later, following their conference in London, the three Western foreign ministers announced the basic principles for restoring German unity and decided at the same time that "the first step" toward this goal "should be the holding throughout Germany of free elections to a Constituent Assembly."[19] Thus the Kremlin was unable to get around the concept of free elections, for it had become the cornerstone on which any further movement on the German question was based.

The concept was also used to block all initiatives made by the Eastern side from then on. And it provided the reason both Adenauer and the SPD gave for their "strategy of rejecting" any initiatives made by the SED. Waldemar Besson pointed out that this demand for free elections "was inappropriate to the actual power position in central Europe. It threatened to take away the Soviet Union's spoils of war, without even touching on the question of compensation. This unquestionably made an impression in the West, but it was certainly not the first sign of a feasible policy toward the East."[20] At this time in London, it was secretly asserted with satisfaction that "Adenauer is probably the best chancellor we can get" to carry out Western policy.[21]

In the autumn of 1950, the decision in principle to rearm the Federal Republic precipitated some movement on the German question. The foreign ministers of the Eastern bloc nations made the first move, at their conference in Prague on October 20–21, by demanding the immediate conclusion of a peace treaty with Germany and the withdrawal of all occupying troops one year later. On November 30, Minister President Grotewohl of the GDR proposed in writing to Adenauer that an "all-German constitutional council composed equally of representatives from East and West Germany" should prepare "to establish a sovereign, democratic, and peaceful all-German provisional government."[22] On November 3 and again on December 15, the Soviet Union demanded that a foreign ministers' conference be convoked to discuss the demilitarization of Germany.

Adenauer could easily reject Grotewohl's offer by referring to "free elections" (memorandum from January 15, 1951), but the Western foreign ministers consented to a preliminary conference of deputy foreign ministers that was to meet in Paris and develop an agenda for a possible foreign ministers' conference. At that time, Foreign Secretary Bevin was as displeased as his French colleagues about American pressure to rearm the Federal Republic. He even considered using rearmament as a card in future four-power negotiations,[23] but he did not pursue these thoughts any further because this was no longer an issue as far as the Americans were concerned. On March 9, 1951, Bevin resigned from his post for reasons of health. Four days before, the preliminary conference had begun in Paris; in the course of this conference the British came over to the American side. The result was a strategy paper of June 1.[24] As described in this paper, the Western powers' goal was to steer a course that would safeguard West Germany from communism and thereby protect their own position in Europe, but that would neither be nor appear to be negative in character. Following an analysis of Soviet policy, four possibilities for reunifying Germany were discussed and rejected in turn:

1. Germany could not enter into any military alliances with foreign powers nor have any national armed forces except the police; the occupying troops were to be withdrawn. The conclusion: "Any plan which leads to a neutralised, demilitarised and unoccupied Germany must be ruled out," because it was feared Germany would not in fact be neutral for long. Germany would not be poised between equal forces: "The West is on the defensive. The East is aggressive." The Germans, although mostly anti-Communist, had less will to resist Communism than, for example, the British, both because the menace of the Soviet Union was nearer at hand, and because "years of occupation have sapped their moral courage." Militarily, the plan would immediately deprive the Western powers not only of a German defense contribution, which they believed to be essential to their own security, but also of a depth of territory between the Rhine and the Elbe, which was of military importance; apart from ordinary strategic and tactical considerations, the West would lose valuable radar warnings of enemy action and great intelligence opportunities. The situation would be even worse by the time Germany had been completely taken over by the Russians.

2. As in 1, however, a gendarmerie or a small army for internal defense was conceded. The conclusion: "We should be doing precisely what we have said we would never do . . . , namely, letting Germany have a national armed force of her own and *an armed force of a peculiar isolated and independent character.*" As the whole background of current Western policy was to make the Germans good citizens not by solitary confinement but by letting them become members of a good club, this plan was rejected because it "would enable Germany to balance between East and West, and to sell herself to the highest bidder, with the likelihood that a new and dangerous situation would arise."

3. The "Austrian solution," that is, a demilitarized Germany united on Western terms under a central government, but still divided into Eastern and Western zones and occupied by Soviet and Allied troops with a minimum of four-power control. The conclusion: This plan would not be accepted by the Germans as a long-term solution. The Germans wished to become masters in their own house. A central German government in Berlin would be encircled by Soviet troops, and unable to exert authority in the Eastern zone. The plan would entail the loss of the German contribution to Western defense. It had, there-

fore, "serious disadvantages and nothing to recommend it in comparison with the present system."

4. A variant of 3: there would be an unoccupied federal zone including Berlin; in this zone, a German government could function freely, without direct pressure from the occupying powers; such a government should have no troops at its disposal, and military alliances with other powers would not be allowed. The unoccupied area would gradually be enlarged to extend the area of freedom until all the occupying troops were finally withdrawn. This plan had much the same disadvantages as the previous plan; that is, the central government would still not be able to exercise jurisdiction throughout the country, and the Communists would continue to fasten their tentacles on the Eastern area. The plan did not face up to the question of what was to happen when the time came for the troops to be withdrawn completely. Neither did it take account of the West's predicament if, in the process of withdrawal, the Soviets, by some means not obviously illegal, obtained control of the central government. The Western powers might find themselves compelled either to hand over the Ruhr to a Communist government or to act in plain breach of their formal agreements. The conclusion: "This scheme also has no advantages to offer by comparison with the existing system."

The preliminary conference in Paris failed because no side was seriously interested in altering the status quo. This changed in the autumn of 1951 when a breakthrough was attained at the negotiations for the European Defense Community. If developments in the West were to be interrupted or stopped, then better offers needed to come from the East. The first came on September 15; it was the most extensive offer ever made by East Berlin. Grotewohl expressly addressed the demand for free elections. He no longer spoke of equal representation from East and West Germany. Now the slogan was, "Germans at one table." The first task of an all-German advisory council would be to schedule free elections for a national assembly, rather than to conclude a peace treaty, as had previously been demanded. All democratic parties and organizations should have the right to nominate candidates and to form coalitions. Without a doubt, this was an offer of definite import, and it aroused considerable apprehension among the Western allies.[25]

On September 27, Adenauer countered with fourteen election regulations for all-German elections and demanded that, instead of an all-German advisory council, a neutral international commission certify that the necessary requirements for these elections had been met.[26]

Surprisingly, on October 10, the GDR government accepted the majority of the fourteen points; however, it was considered advisable to discuss international control in the all-German conference. With the help of the Western powers, Adenauer then killed the East German initiative. In a speech in Berlin on October 6, he had already presented additional stipulations for reunification by demanding the inclusion of the territories east of the Oder and Neisse rivers.[27] He had also asked the Federal Constitutional Court to ban the German Communist party (KPD) and the right-extremist Socialist Reich's party (SRP)—although he simultaneously demanded that all parties be guaranteed participation in the all-German elections. Now a United Nations commission was to "carry out immediately a simultaneous investigation in the Federal Republic of Germany, in Berlin, and in the Soviet Zone of Germany to ascertain and report whether conditions in these areas are such as to make possible the holding of genuinely free and secret elections throughout these areas" (Point 2: "Resolution on the Appointment of an International Commission to Investigate the Possibility of Free German Elections").[28]

This was a cleverly carried-out propaganda maneuver and was viewed as such by the Western side. In the West, no one expected the GDR to grant entry to the commission. To ascertain that the necessary prerequisites for free all-German elections did not exist in the GDR, one did not need a United Nations commission; everyone knew this already. No one less than George Kennan later severely criticized [the idea behind] this commission. And when Adenauer, looking back in his memoirs, characterized precisely this decision to grant or not grant approval to the commission in connection with the Stalin Note as "decisive," as "a truly serious step toward peace by the Soviet Union," his description is not convincing. On the contrary, it makes it clear that something else was at stake, namely, preventing serious talks with the Soviet Union. French Foreign Minister Robert Schuman told his British colleague Anthony Eden in Paris that Adenauer needed to speak out publicly in favor of reunification even though he did not think much of the idea, because it was certain that the SPD would attain a majority in all-German elections.[29]

As expected, the GDR government rejected the United Nations commission as interference in their internal affairs. As the GDR press put it, a venerable, civilized people such as the Germans did not have to allow Brazilians and Pakistanis to verify its capacity for conducting free elections.[30] And on February 13, 1952, the GDR government asked the Kremlin to "speed up the conclusion of a peace treaty with Germany."[31]

CHAPTER FOUR

LONDON, PARIS, AND
THE FIRST NOTE
"A Serious but Very Dangerous
Attempt to Settle the
German Question"

When the note lay on the table on March 10, Western observers agreed that this was an initial Soviet reaction to the decisions made at the NATO conference in Lisbon on February 20–25 as well as to the looming military and political integration of the Federal Republic into the Western alliance. The crucial question was whether the note was only a tactical maneuver designed to provide the opponents of integration policy with some ammunition, to awaken false hopes, and thus to torpedo the policy, or whether it signaled a fundamental change in Soviet policy. The answer to this question would also settle the question about the goals of the Western powers discussed in the previous chapter.

In a preliminary analysis on March 11, Denis Allen, head of the European section in the British Foreign Office, and Frank Roberts, head of the German section, came to this conclusion: the main object of the note was to delay and, if possible, prevent the incorporation of the

Federal Republic into the Western defense system; the note was designed to appeal to those sections of opinion in Germany, and also in Western Europe generally, that had doubts about the wisdom of a German association with a Western defense before the prospects of agreement with Soviet Russia on German unity had been fully explored. Because of this assessment, Allen and Roberts considered it necessary to handle the note so as to avoid playing into the hands of these critics. This meant "playing for time," at least until the European Defense Community Treaty and the Bonn Convention were signed, since their signing had been an absolute priority from the beginning. Perhaps, Allen and Roberts suggested, the Western powers should consider agreeing to early four-power negotiations, in the hope of demonstrating "reasonably quickly" that agreement was not possible. *Thereafter*, negotiations with the Federal Republic could be resumed. However, they agreed that such a course would clearly be hazardous, and that it was most unlikely that the United States government would agree to it.[1]

What is both remarkable about this analysis and especially important to our discussion of "German maneuverability" is the following: if two of the highest officials in the Foreign Office did not exclude the possibility of four-power negotiations *before* signing the European Defense Community Treaty and the Bonn Convention, then a similar German request would scarcely have meant the end of the Western treaties. Adenauer believed, as he later put it, that such a request would offend the Western powers, thus jeopardizing their willingness to cooperate.[2] In 1982, Grewe expressed the same view: "In this situation, everything seemed to indicate that postponing the treaty negotiations would seriously bring into question whether they could ever be concluded at all—especially if this postponement were occasioned by a German initiative that aroused mistrust in the West."[3]

When Gerstenmaier emphasized in 1981 that the German side "could certainly have suggested a foreign ministers' conference; that lay within our options,"[4] then in hindsight we must agree with him. Even the Americans at least discussed taking the offensive when responding to the first note so as to force the Soviets to lay their cards on the table (see chapter 5). Thirty-three years later, in an interview with the author, Sir Frank Roberts confirmed this view:

1. If Adenauer, by referring to the domestic situation, had expressed a wish to explore the note, if he had pushed for a four-power conference to clarify Soviet intentions at the negotiating table, the

Western powers would probably have first tried to dissuade him. In the end, however, they would not have denied him his wish, indeed could not have denied it to him, in view of their public proclamations concerning reunification, without running the danger of losing the rationale for their German policy in the Federal Republic.

2. In any case, such a wish would not have brought an end to the policy of integration.[5]

The alternative dramatically formulated by Bucerius, "With the West— or with the East!" thus did not really apply. "Distrust of the Western powers," "sitting between two chairs," "endangering the treaties with the West"—none of these were the real issue then, and they are not the real issue today. What *is* critical is that Adenauer, for the reasons already discussed, did not want any negotiations. Once he had made this unmistakably clear to the high commissioners on March 11, there was no need for the Foreign Office, which had immediately seized the initiative in formulating a Western response, to pursue this possibility any further. It is also not surprising that Foreign Minister Eden— referring to Adenauer's reaction—did not mention this possibility in the cabinet meeting on the morning of March 12. Here he described the note as an "important advance on any offer" previously made by the Soviet Union. The note was an "astute maneuver" designed to wreck the policy of integration. But, he conceded, it might reflect the Soviets' "sincere desire" for German reunification. Continued negotiations for the European Defense Community Treaty and the Bonn Convention must be the Western strategy. Then perhaps the Soviets might come forward with a more satisfactory offer. The test of their sincerity would be their willingness to agree to the holding of free elections, under independent supervision, throughout Germany; and it was perhaps significant that there was no mention of this in their present proposals.[6]

The ambassadors of the United States and France in London agreed with the assessment of the situation Eden presented on the afternoon of March 12: the note demonstrated the success of Western policy; now the Soviet Union might be prepared to pay a higher price than before in order to prevent the integration of the Federal Republic into the Western world. While one could not regard the price now offered, even at its face value, as in any way satisfactory, one could reasonably regard this development as encouraging. Adenauer's "robust reaction" was gratifying, but it did not follow that the Soviet offer would not attract the German Socialists and "neutralist" elements. A Western response must therefore assist the Federal Republic by addressing the criticism of the opposition. Eden did not yet exclude the possibility of the Soviet Union's offering free, all-German elections and agreeing to the establishment of a truly free government in Berlin. If this should occur, he foresaw new difficulties because this would not necessarily mean that the Soviet Union would then proceed to a peace treaty on acceptable terms. The West might be left with a solution no better than the position in Austria. Only a few hours before, the French ambassador had presented the same argument. However, Roberts pointed out that, if that were to happen, the Soviets would not then have achieved their other objective of getting American troops out of Germany and Western Europe.[7] Even in the Quai d'Orsay, no one was convinced at this point that the note was anything more than a disruptive maneuver.[8]

On March 13, the French did not exclude the possibility of agreeing to a four-power conference. The Western powers should try to define as precisely as possible the conditions on which they would be willing to take part in such a conference. Among these conditions might be the signing of the Austrian State Treaty[9] by the Soviet government and the previous admission of the United Nations commission into the Eastern zone of Germany.[10] Only one day later, their assessment of the situation looked completely different. In Paris, the most important concern then became avoiding a situation in which free elections would take place, since they would mean that an all-German government, probably under Schumacher's leadership, would be established in Berlin and that thereafter progress on a peace treaty would be held up, as [had been the case] in Austria (Sir William Strang's note: "This is important."). This would mean losing all the advantages of the European Defense Community and of Western integration policy; in return, a united Germany would be increasingly under Soviet pressure and influence. In view of public opinion in Germany, the response to the Soviet note must of course concentrate on free elections and unity, but it should be quite clear that the Western powers could not accept a unified Germany, even with genuinely free elections, until they knew that a peace treaty satisfactory to them would also be concluded shortly. Then the French mentioned those aspects of the Soviet note about which they had special reservations:

1. *The Saar.* Poland would have the Oder–Neisse frontier, but France would lose the Saar.

2. *Neutralization clause.* This would of course mean the complete abandonment of the European Defense Community and of all Western integration policy.

3. *Military clause.* Here a new element had been introduced in that

not only were occupying troops to be withdrawn, but foreign military bases were to be liquidated as well. The really essential point in regard to both the military clause and the neutralization clause was that there was no provision whatever for control.

4. *Economic conditions.* These were perhaps even more dangerous, since Germany would be left completely free to trade with the East, whereas other West European countries had accepted important limitations on their trade with the Communist world (Sir William Strang's note: "So is this"). Germany would rapidly build herself up into a more formidable economic unit then ever before by trading on an immense scale with her natural hinterland in Eastern Europe and also in Russia and China. Furthermore, there would be nothing to stop Germany from setting up an immense military industry to supply the armies of the Soviet Union and the satellites, even if her military production for equipping her own army were kept at a relatively low level.

As Frank Roberts noted on March 14:

> In other words, the Quai d'Orsay fear that the effect of the Soviet proposals would be to produce a rich and economically strong Germany which would however be militarily dominated by the Soviet Union and which would also be under Soviet economic dominance for the reasons set out above. On the whole the Quai d'Orsay had modified their original view and now thought the Soviet proposals were much more than a tactical move and were a serious but very dangerous attempt to settle the German question.[11]

This led Eden to comment that he had held the view all along that "the Soviets are sincere in these proposals because, though there is danger in them, they would on balance suit them well."

If that were so, then the envisioned integration of the Federal Republic—and the continuing division of Germany—was then, as before, the better solution for the Western powers. Negotiations with the Soviet Union that might endanger integration must certainly not take place. It was no longer a matter of the repeatedly posed demand for free elections. The risk of the Soviet Union's agreeing to these elections appeared too great even to the British. If that happened, there would be an all-German government, but the Soviet Union would then be able to delay the next step; concluding a peace treaty. The West would then have lost the Federal Republic as an ally "without getting anything in return."[12] After speaking with Jean Sauvagnargues, head of the European section at the Quai d'Orsay, the American ambassador reported to Washington from Paris on March 19:

While he believes that Soviets would much rather avoid admitting a UN commission (and their reference to "earliest possible" establishment of an all-German government attests to their desire to avoid a way-station to unity), Sauvagnargues does not exclude the possibility that the Soviets decided they can risk the establishment of an "interim unified government" even on the basis of free elections, as the best means to interpose effective and prolonged delays to Western integration. Once such a government has been established, somewhat on the Austrian pattern, the four powers could then talk peace treaty until the cows come home, Western European integration would be effectively delayed, and the Soviets would retain the capability of undoing the unity, as well as freedom in their zone, whenever it suited their convenience.[13]

And what would happen if Kurt Schumacher, the leader of the SPD, were to form an all-German government? William Strang had referred to this problem a few days earlier. At the bottom of a draft of a response viewed as a basis for three-power deliberations in Paris, he noted that in the draft response emphasis had been placed on free elections, as had been consistently advocated in the past. If the Russians were to concede fully to the West's conditions in this sphere, which he considered unlikely, then the result of a free all-German election would probably be to establish a Schumacher government, owing to the weakness of the CDU in East Germany. Such a government would probably reverse Adenauer's policy of integration with the West and would pursue a policy of neutrality and maneuvering between East and West. From this, Strang concluded rather resignedly: "We have no alternative but to take this risk." But Eden doubted this. His notes make his concerns clear. In the margin, he wrote: "Is this really so? Are there not other conditions we could add? E.g., Austria? I don't suggest mentioning that to our allies at present." He added that these notes were to apply only in the event that the Soviets really wanted to pursue a new policy. And as if searching for confirmation from his colleagues, he asked: "If they could realize it would it not have important advantages for them?"[14]

Eden's concerns were unfounded. The French shared his views; moreover, there were numerous other requirements. First, the Oder–Neisse line; this was a "fundamental weakness of [the] Russian case," according to the British ambassador in Moscow, although it was a "delicate" issue for the West as well. Eden commented that the ambassador "may have given us a good card here."[15] Indeed, the card was so good that it appeared as Point 5 in the response dated March 25. At first, Paris also wanted to make concluding a state treaty with Austria a condition in the response; but this was later dropped as too excessive, especially since the U.S. State Department wanted the response to focus solely on the issue of free elections.

More important was Point 3 of the response: freedom of negotiation for the all-German government. The demand that this government should be as free before a peace treaty was concluded as after to enter into alliances in keeping with the principles and goals of the United Nations (and according to Western interpretation this included the European Defense Community and NATO) struck at the heart of the Soviet note and was thus certain to be rejected. For the Soviets, the price of relinquishing their spoils of war, the GDR, could not consist of granting an all-German government the right to decide whether all of Germany should join the European Defense Community, possibly with the result that European Defense Community and NATO troops would advance from the Elbe to the Oder. No one could seriously demand this of the Kremlin leaders, since this was precisely what they had hoped to avoid with their proposal. With this seemingly very "democratic" demand for an all-German government's freedom of action, the West was insisting on the Kremlin's capitulation before negotiations were even begun. Under such conditions there would never be an all-German government. In this fashion, the Western powers also solved their own problem: such a government, possibly under Schumacher's leadership, would vote against integration into the Western alliance.

On March 17, Adenauer offered the allies help in making their decision. In speaking to the high commissioners, he first emphasized what he did not want:

1. A four-power conference. It would lead to no results, would last too long, and would slow up progress toward the European Defense Community and the integration of Europe.

2. A purely negative answer. This would have a bad psychological result in Germany. The West should try to show up the Russian note by replying with some precise questions that could be easily understood by the public in the rest of the world. There were two in particular that should be asked: (a) Are the Soviets now prepared to allow the United Nations commission to enter the Soviet zone? (b) What do the Soviets mean when they say that Germany must not enter into any coalitions or military alliances with any country that was at war with Germany? Does this include such projects as the Schuman Plan, the European Defense Community, and the integra-

tion of Europe? At the end of this discussion, the high commission-ers and Adenauer agreed that it was essential that the treaty negoti-ations not be held up, even if the note led to a series of diplomatic exchanges or a conference.[16]

On March 20 and 21, Adenauer met with Schuman, Eden, and Amer-ican Ambassador James Dunn in Paris. In the intervening days, the editorial committee had worked up a draft response. On March 20, Schuman told the chancellor what he and his colleagues thought to be the main points raised by the Soviet note and asked for his views. Adenauer's reply showed "complete agreement" with the general con-tours. The object should be to avoid discussions with the Russians and to press on with the European Defense Community. The reply should be brief, simple, and reasonable and should deal not only with elections but also with frontiers, a German national army, and neutrality. It should be made clear that Germany must be allowed to continue to cooperate in the policy of European integration, that great importance was attached to German unity, but that peace was the whole object of Western policies.

At the meeting on the following day, Adenauer was shown the draft of the response. He was satisfied and made only a couple of comments. The passage concerning the status of the German government seemed obscure, so that a misinterpretation was possible: the German public could infer that the Western powers would entertain the possibility of an Austrian solution. He felt that this point should be made more precise, and elsewhere the positive aspects of future European unity should be emphasized and the negative aspects of forestalling the re-vival of German militarism deemphasized.[17]

CHAPTER FIVE

WASHINGTON AND THE FIRST NOTE

Why No Offensive Strategy?

The Americans' initial reactions to the Soviet note were not unanimous either. Nevertheless, everyone found the German reaction reassuring: Undersecretary Walter Hallstein, one of Adenauer's closest advisers, who spoke at the State Department in Washington on March 11, stated that he was certain that the note would have no effect whatever on the chancellor or other government leaders. They would readily see the loopholes in the note and recognize that it presented no basic change of heart on the part of the Russians.[1] Acheson expressed the same view,[2] although he was "obviously impressed" by the importance of the note: "Its tone was so different from earlier ones." As Acheson told the British ambassador, he was also speculating on what move the Russians might make if the response to the present note did not bring them what they wanted.[3] In the meantime, the first assessments of the situation arrived from Bonn, Berlin, Paris, Moscow, and London.

By March 11, McCloy realized that the Soviet note would have "serious and unpredictable repercussions" in the Federal Republic.[4] On the same day, he reported on the preliminary comments made in Bonn,[5] and on March 12, he presented his first analysis after the introductory report from the General Counsel in Hamburg arrived (Axel Springer, the influential West German publisher, declared himself in favor of negotiations—"in the most vigorous manner possible"[6]). He described the initial reactions in the Federal Republic as "gratifyingly level-headed." Fortunately for the Americans, most Germans had few illusions about Russia and bolshevism; nevertheless, the Soviet note could still become dangerous because many Germans who felt strongly on the unity issue, despite their skepticism, would wishfully hope that the Kremlin proposal might "at least be given a try." The Germans' natural tendency to look back over their shoulders at unity as a first priority could intensify and cause a delay in the negotiations concerning integration just when the Americans wanted to quicken the pace. Since this tendency was so deeply rooted and so amorphous, the Germans' initial sane reaction to the note might not remain steady. Should the Western response appear to be negative and to foreclose the possibility of German unity, then the note would come to exercise an appeal it did not now possess: it could seriously endanger negotiations concerning integration. McCloy then made some suggestions for a response note, placing the emphasis on free elections.[7]

An American representative on the high commission, Cecil Lyon, reported from Berlin that the general feeling was that the Soviets were primarily concerned about preventing the Federal Republic from rearming and joining the Western alliance, a feeling that he shared. People were not in agreement, however, on the question of whether and how far the Soviets would go toward making concessions to Western demands in order to reach a final agreement on the unification of Germany. It seemed probable that the Soviets would decide to retire from East Germany, if at all, only if induced to make a decision based on one or both of the following suppositions: (1) that the integration of West Germany with Western Europe and its progressive rearmament would represent a serious threat to Soviet expansion and possibly eventually to Soviet security, and that this process could be stopped only by an agreement providing for some kind of "neutralization" of a united Germany and for the withdrawal of American and West European forces behind German borders; and (2) that the withdrawal of both East and West from a unified Germany would later be followed by a gradual integration of all Germany into the Communist orbit, presumably through the utilization of time-tested techniques of Communist penetration, a highly organized use of propaganda, subversion, and the manipulation of "mass organizations." In this endeavor, the Soviets would probably rely on the fact that the economies of Germany and Eastern Europe were naturally complementary and on the historical attraction of authoritarian forms of government for the German people.[8]

Three days later, Lyon reported there was evidence that the Soviets might be aiming at something different. If the four-power negotiations were to fail, the Kremlin would have a legal and moral basis for (1) making the Western powers responsible for the division of Germany, (2) drawing up a peace treaty with an all-German national committee, and/or (3) openly proceeding with an expanded buildup of armed forces for the GDR.[9]

On March 16, McCloy reexamined the note in connection with Grotewohl's speech.[10] In his view, most political observers in Bonn considered the note an element of Soviet obstructionist politics. Yet a few spoke of "a more far-reaching change in Kremlin policy—a serious offer of a Rapallo in reverse." Moreover, since the Kremlin had felt it necessary to lay its political cards on the table, those in the high commission speculated that the Kremlin must have estimated that the military reconstruction of Western Europe had already "progressed even further than we think." If that were true, then this was obviously a development of major significance, the interpretation of which extended far beyond the high commission's province.[11] The American embassy in Moscow ruled out any such development. On March 16, the embassy staff dismissed the note as propaganda. They found it difficult to believe that the Soviet Union would permit free elections to take place in the GDR and thus relinquish authority there, since without controlling the GDR it could not attain its goals in Europe. In the embassy staff's view, Soviet policy had traditionally been to hold onto what they had rather than to engage in trades.[12]

The American draft of the response note[13] corresponded to the British draft[14] to a great extent and also underscored free elections. The Policy Planning Staff of the U.S. State Department did not support this draft. Instead, they proposed an alternative response to the Soviet note. In their view, the Russians had formulated the first note to enable them to attain at least their minimum goal with the second note: blocking the European Defense Community for the time being by involving the Western powers in negotiations. In the second note, they could easily make proposals that would look good enough to embarrass the Western powers without committing the Russians in any way that would embarrass them. The danger was that the Western powers would not be able to avoid negotiations without appearing to be the real obstruction-ists of German reunification and a German peace treaty. The worst outcome would be to be trapped into discussions both on the election issue and on peace terms, yet to be blocked meanwhile from carrying through the European Defense Community Treaty and to have ex-tracted no price from the Russians in turn.

To prevent this from occurring, the Policy Planning Staff argued for an offensive strategy: beating the Soviets at their own game. Agreement to negotiate on the issue of free elections should depend on satisfying very specific conditions, and there should be no doubt that fulfilling these conditions would result in political consequences for the Soviets' position in East Germany. In this way, the Soviets' bluff could be clearly exposed. There were nine chances in ten that they were not prepared to permit free political activity in their zone: "No matter how they screamed, the significance of their refusal would not be lost on anyone." Why not frankly say, the Policy Planning Staff asked, that we believe that the Russians are bluffing; that they are trying to block the European Defense Community by causing confusion; that the reunifi-cation of Germany has always been a major aim of Western policy; that, if the Russians are ready to permit free elections and allow a democratic all-German government, there is no reason why they can-not establish the conditions necessary for free elections at once; that, if the Russians have changed their policy, this is a tribute to the success of Western policy; and that the West should keep the pressure on by proceeding with the European Defense Community, especially since the Russian proposals are probably only a trick designed to block the community and perpetuate the division of Germany.

The Policy Planning Staff could not gain acceptance of this strategy. In their assessment, the staff had pointed out the probable conse-quences in the event that the Russians were not bluffing and were really prepared to pay, if necessary, the price of free elections in order to block West Germany's entrance into the European Defense Com-munity. If this were the case, so the staff's summary ran, "there is no way of avoiding the necessity for dealing with the problem of a unified Germany and for readjusting our European policy."[15]

Meanwhile, the American ambassador in Paris had let the British and French convince him that the issue was no longer solely one of free elections. The conditions under which the West was prepared to nego-tiate should be made clear to the Kremlin from the outset.[16]

CHAPTER SIX

OPPOSITION TO REUNIFICATION IN THE STATE DEPARTMENT: MARCH 25–APRIL 9

On March 25, three identical Western notes were presented in Moscow.[1] Foreign Minister A. Y. Vyshinskii received the representatives of the Western powers individually and spoke to each of them for about thirty minutes. In these conversations, he clarified three points:

1. The Soviet rejection of the United Nations commission remained.
2. Germany could not join NATO; its membership would be incompatible with the principles of the United Nations.
3. The frontiers adopted at Potsdam were definitive and final.

This third point was made with "emphasis, and even some heat."[2]

After March 25, speculation concerning Soviet intentions continued. The French ambassador in London, René Massigli, was now convinced that the Soviets sincerely wanted to negotiate. On March 26, Eden endorsed this view; indeed, Eden had always considered this a possibility but wanted to wait for the next Soviet note to be certain. Eden also considered Vyshinskii's conversations when the notes were delivered "an unusual experience on such an occasion."[3]

In Moscow, the Americans at the embassy realized that, as far as the Soviets were concerned, they had made the Germans the most attractive offer possible: "Unity plus national army plus peace seems hard to beat." And the possibility could no longer be excluded that the Soviets might even make concessions concerning the Oder–Neisse border, as the "ultimate carrot to lead the German donkey over the hump."[4]

Russian experts in Washington perceived an important and fundamental shift in the Kremlin's approach to Germany, which had been developing for some time.[5] On March 29, McCloy evidently felt that the Kremlin had provided the Germans with a surprisingly clear-cut offer, even given the well-known Soviet semantics, against which the Germans could measure the advantages and disadvantages of following the present course of contractual agreements and integration with the West.

McCloy did not rule out the possibility that, as its next step, the Kremlin might press vigorously to split Adenauer off from the rest of Germany, Germany from Western Europe, and Western Europe from the United States.[6] As McCloy stated in a second telegram on March 29, some of Adenauer's advisers saw a parallel between the present situation and 1939, when the Hitler–Stalin pact was signed. Adenauer was aware of the challenge this posed, but he firmly believed it was up to Germany to prove her loyalty to the West by flatly rejecting the Soviet note and expediting the conclusion of the treaties with the West. However, he was constrained by the fact that a flat rejection would give the appearance of forsaking Germany's own national interests in the interests of Western Europe, or, as one cabinet member (Kaiser) put it, of being "more American than the Americans." A few "soft-headed nationalists," such as Franz Blücher, and some representatives of the left wing of the CDU, including Kaiser and Heinrich von Brentano, recommended a slowing down rather than a speeding up of current negotiations; they opposed a flat rejection and urged further exploration of the Soviet offer before a final commitment to the West was made.[7]

In Washington, the Policy Planning Staff of the State Department explored various possible options for the next Soviet step. Interestingly enough, one point in their draft document later appeared in almost the same wording in the Soviet response. The Policy Planning Staff expected that the Soviets would reject the United Nations commission as they had before and would instead propose that a four-power investigating group be set up and that simultaneously discussions be initiated to prepare an election. The Russians would probably not suggest this unless they had previously decided to proceed with free elections, although they probably hoped that these elections could be delayed for a long time. If the Russian rejoinder to the Western reply involved action pointing toward free elections, "we will have to give more weight than we now do to the possibility that there has been a change in Russian policy." If that was the case, then "we want to make them pay as high a price as possible since we will be forced to give up a line of development in which we have made a large investment." The Russians would then have to be compelled either to abandon their game or to go quickly all the way to free elections. The second Western note should bring home to them that "the unification game, if it is to be played at all, will be played seriously and to a conclusion."[8]

What form this game might take was the issue that leading officials in the State Department attempted to clarify when discussing the situation on April 1. This discussion revealed both very substantial differences of opinion concerning the advisability of reunification at all and considered uncertainty concerning the fundamental goals of the United States in Europe.

With regard to the immediate question of whether they should favor reunification at the present time, Paul Nitze, director of the Policy Planning Staff, made clear that they had put themselves on record in favor of free elections leading to a unified Germany, and that they could not withdraw from this position. As the discussions began, Nitze and the Russian expert, Charles Bohlen, agreed that the preferred United States solution of the German situation would be a unified Germany within the European Defense Community, although both were very doubtful whether the French would accept such a solution. There was no discussion of how France would feel about a united Germany outside the European Defense Community, but presumably the French would have very grave reservations about this, too, unless very strict controls were maintained on Germany's military potential.

Perry Laukhuff, head of the German section, and Jeffrey Lewis, his deputy, took no exception to the objective of a united Germany within the European Defense Community, but they made it clear that their doubts about the feasibility of accomplishing the objective placed them in opposition to German unity and the preliminary step of free elections at the present time. The German section's position seemed to be that it was better to have Western Germany in the European Defense Community than to gamble on a unified Germany that would be free to stay out of, or to quit, the community. Discussion of the abstract

desirability of German unification produced less rather than more conviction that a unified Germany was a desirable goal.

For Bohlen, the primary concern was the danger of a united Germany
in a divided Europe: he envisioned German domination of the continent or a rapprochement with the Soviet Union. In his view, Stalin's
offer was really directed at the right-wing industrialists who supported
Adenauer rather than at the Social Democrats. It was the industrialists
whom the Soviet Union could tempt with markets stretching from
Eastern Europe to the Pacific (including China), markets that it would
be very difficult for Germany to duplicate in the West. Nitze shared
some of Bohlen's fears of a "unified Germany in a divided Europe," but
he preferred what he regarded as a more "aggressive" interpretation of
the problem, that is, that the unification of Germany would tend to
accelerate the unification of Europe as a whole.

The participants were also uncertain about what the West Germans
actually wanted, that is, how they were likely to respond to possible
Soviet and Western moves. Both Nitze and John Ferguson, the deputy
director of the Policy Planning Staff, believed that the West Germans
were primarily interested in Germany unity. Ferguson believed that if
the West Germans were faced with the simple choice of West German
integration into Western Europe or unification of all Germany, they
would take the second. Nitze agreed that the Soviets could block the
contractual arrangements and German participation in the European
Defense Community if they were genuinely willing to establish a free
and united Germany—which would mean for them "liquidating the
entire East German investment." He thought it unlikely, however, that
the West Germans would be confronted with a simple choice between
integration and reunification. He foresaw a choice between reunification in the near future and an immediate integration that would not
preclude subsequent reunification. In his view and in that of the German section, when faced with this choice the West Germans would
take the latter course.

Ferguson was very doubtful of this analysis. Intelligence reports had
convinced him that the Germans wanted unity above all else and
would buy what appeared to them a bona fide Soviet offer. He felt it
would be very difficult to pursue effectively the parallel propaganda
course suggested by Ambassador Philip Jessup pursuant to the Nitze
analysis, that is, simultaneous emphasis on German unity and German
integration with the West. Bohlen, on the other hand, was inclined to
presume that the West Germans' desire for reunification might perhaps
have been overestimated. He asked himself whether the West Germans

were not more skeptical of Soviet good faith on the reunification issue than had previously been assumed. In the end, the group agreed on the following tactics:

1. We are going ahead on integration.

2. If the Soviet Union is genuinely prepared to permit free elections and the consequent establishment of a unified Germany, we are prepared to let the ultimate all-German government decide whether it wishes to continue its adherence to the integration program. [In speaking of "integration," Bohlen had in mind not only the EDC (European Defense Community), but also the Schuman Plan.]

3. On the question of possible talks with the Soviet Union about Germany, there was general agreement that they should be avoided if possible.

4. There was general agreement that we should step up our propaganda in Germany in accordance with whatever substantive objectives we agree upon. It was specifically suggested by Bohlen, pursuant to his analysis outlined above, that we lay increasing stress on the dangers to Germany of the Soviet armies and the need to counter those dangers by accelerating the integration program.

Jessup suggested trying to emphasize the idea that integration was in no way incompatible with German reunification. At this point, John Ferguson repeated his doubts "that we could effectively persuade the Germans of this secondary proposition . . . and that it was very difficult for us to make effective propaganda on the basis of a position about which we are not ourselves convinced."[9]

In keeping with this resolution, however, posters appeared overnight in the Federal Republic propagandizing against the Stalin Note. They lacked nothing in clarity. (One poster, entitled "Today, the German National Army—Tomorrow, a German Soviet Republic," was published by the Liberation Committee for the Victims of Totalitarian Despotism; a second—"Moscow wants the Ruhr territory for Soviet armaments. Therefore, Germany is to be isolated from the West. Never!"— came from the Combat Patrol Against Bolshevik Corruption).[10] In addition, the United States now pressed for a rapid conclusion to the negotiations concerning integration. The treaties with the West were to be signed in the first half of May. On April 12, Acheson set the date: May 9. Because of the upcoming congressional vote on defense appropriations, if the treaties could not be signed in May, their ratification could be expected only in early 1953, if at all.[11]

CHAPTER 7

THE SECOND SOVIET NOTE, APRIL 9, 1952

The American Offer to Negotiate and the Rejection by Adenauer

On the evening of April 9, Foreign Minister Vyshinskii gave the Western representatives in Moscow the reply to their note from March 25. On the matter of free elections, the Soviet response stated: "Recognition on the part of the Governments of the USSR, United States of America, England, and France of the necessity of conducting free all-German elections will create the full possibility of conducting such elections in the nearest future." Deciding whether the prerequisites for such elections existed "could be carried out by a commission formed by the Four Powers fulfilling occupation functions in Germany."[1] Neither the British chargé d'affaires Paul Grey nor his American colleague H. Cumming were successful in obtaining explanatory information from Vyshinskii.[2] Grey viewed this proposal as propaganda, as he had the previous Soviet offer. It confirmed his earlier presumption that the Soviet government did not want elections before the negotiation of a peace treaty.[3]

In his first analysis, Brooke Turner from the British Foreign Office examined the crux of the problem: the all-German government's freedom to negotiate. According to the Western view, such a government was not a sovereign power if it was denied the right to join military alliances. The Soviet government held the opposite view that the withholding of this right was entirely compatible with the full sovereignty of an all-German government. This note was the Soviet Union's attempt to maintain the initiative in the German question. To seize the initiative, the West would need to make its own proposals, but this was at present "rather an embarrassing matter."[4]

Immediately after being informed of the note, Adenauer requested a meeting with the high commissioners. Since François-Poncet was not authorized by his government to participate in this talk, the high commissioners agreed that Kirkpatrick, as chairman, should be the only one to see Adenauer. This meeting occurred on April 11. As with the first note, Adenauer was eager to make his views on the new note and on an appropriate response immediately clear to the Western powers. In the first place, he did not regard the note as very clever; it was aimed primarily at German public opinion. For this reason, in the response, it would be well to emphasize at the outset the intention of the Western powers to promote the reunification of Germany in freedom. Equally important, they must state that they were fully prepared to hold a four-power conference. However, three issues must first be settled:

1. The future full sovereignty of Germany with the right to conclude any alliances she pleased.
2. Germany's defense forces.
3. Germany's frontiers.

Interesting here is the position to which Adenauer now relegated the all-German elections: in view of German public opinion, this issue should be mentioned only at the end of the response note. He rejected four-power control of the elections as a farce. The opinion of the Western powers was well known and would be in clear conflict with that of the Russians.[5]

Significantly, Adenauer neglected to mention this discussion in his *Erinnerungen*. That this discussion did not fail to have an effect is apparent from the British Foreign Office's first analysis of the Soviet note. At the Foreign Office, the general opinion was that the note was designed primarily to delay and impede Western plans for the association of Germany with the common defense. It consisted mainly of a reiteration of the proposals in the first note.

The main new point was the statement about free all-German elections, but the Soviets had still not committed themselves to the holding of elections before the conclusion of a peace treaty. Apparently, their goal was first to conclude a peace treaty and then to form a provisional all-German government not based on free elections. Consequently, the West should proceed with its present policy of trying to secure the signature and subsequent ratification of the European Defense Community Treaty and the Bonn Convention, and "we must so handle the Soviet Note as to encourage Germany not only to sign but also to ratify these agreements." This meant the West had to be careful not to close the door on four-power discussions on the reunification of Germany. But such negotiations should be avoided until after the treaties were signed; perhaps negotiations could take place in June or July. Until the treaties were signed, the object was to "play for time." The response note, like the Soviet note, should take full account of German opinion. And in so doing, Adenauer's suggestions should be followed so far as possible. The only question was whether one should give such a secondary place, as he suggested, to the question of free elections. Elections were the West's first essential condition and would have to form the main item on the agenda of any four-power discussion: "We must therefore keep them in the forefront."[6]

On April 16, Adenauer again addressed the high commissioners to elaborate upon the views he had expressed on April 11. The first question was Point 7 of the Soviet draft of a peace treaty from March 10, which demanded the "exclusion of a United Germany from any coalition." For Adenauer, this plainly meant both the European Defense Community and the Schuman Plan, but he believed the Russians should be forced to state this fact openly: "Too many simpletons in Germany would find some specious attractions in the Soviet Note until it could be shown in concrete terms what it meant." Once again, he discussed the United Nations commission that was to inquire into the conditions for holding all-German elections (and he again expressed his support for this commission). What would happen if the majority of the members of this commission found that conditions in the Russian zone made free elections impossible? Perhaps the West could ask the Russians specifically whether, whatever commission might make the inquiry, they would be prepared to modify those conditions so as to make them comply with what the commission regarded as essential for free elections.

The chancellor added that there was a risk the public would get the impression that the initiative and the more generous policy were on the Soviet side. They appeared to be offering something constructive. The Western response, therefore, must not appear merely to be turning it down in a negative and obstructive way. The West should take the offensive, put some color into the reply, and show "on which side freedom lay."

At the conclusion of the discussion, François-Poncet—who was irritated by being obliged to discuss the note with the chancellor at all—asked Adenauer what impression he thought would be made on the Social Democrats if they felt that the Western allies, by rushing ahead with their negotiations with the federal government, had "burnt Germany's boats too hastily" before having really proved that the latest Soviet proposals were insincere. This would indeed make the chancellor's position very difficult, and it would certainly make the position of the French government difficult, too. The chancellor must have observed how closely the latest Soviet note corresponded to the position now taken up by Schumacher. He almost wondered if there was not some deliberate connivance. This was the perfect theme for Adenauer: "a bait to which the Chancellor always rises," as Kirkpatrick reported to London.

Adenauer immediately replied that he had for a long time noticed with distress the closer and closer approximation of the SPD's position in foreign policy to that of the Soviet government. He added that he was even more disturbed by a feeling that a part of the British Labour Party and a part of the French Socialist Party were moving in the same direction. As for the too hasty burning of boats, he was sure negotiations with the Western powers must be successfully concluded as rapidly as possible. It followed that the Western powers should not delay their reply too long; otherwise, they would be exposed to the accusation of rushing their own arrangements through while ignoring the Soviet proposals. He thought it would be a good thing if the Western reply could be sent about April 26.[7]

Not without reason did Adenauer hope to relegate free elections to second place in the response note; Stalin's unprecedented consent to the principle of free elections under international control was a clear concession in the eyes of the opposition. With this divergence of opinion, the last tie uniting the government and the opposition in the Federal Republic dissolved. Opponents of integration policy now emphatically demanded four-power negotiations. As Schumacher wrote to Adenauer on April 22, all possibilities should be explored to "determine whether the Soviet note offers an opportunity for finally reunifying Germany in peace." If negotiations revealed that no opportunity existed, "then in any case it will be clear that the Federal Republic did not shy away from the profferred chance for reunification and for a peace settlement in Europe."[8]

With a clear understanding of the implications, Adenauer observed the growing nervousness among the German public and felt himself forced to respond to Schumacher's letter. In an exceptionally adroit manner, he did so on the evening of April 24, in an interview with Ernst Friedländer on Northwest German Radio.

Immediately before his interview, Adenauer called Schumacher, to seek clarification on one or two points and to ask him to delay publication for a while, which Schumacher agreed to do. Then, in the interview, Adenauer covered precisely the same subjects raised by Schumacher and was thus able to minimize the publicity value of the letter had its contents been known to the public before the broadcast. His tone initially differed from all of his numerous previous statements. He favored four-power talks, even though he was convinced that the Soviets were dishonest in proposing the reunification of Germany in freedom. Nevertheless, where the destiny of eighteen million people was at stake, no one should rely on his own opinion. With reference to past unsuccessful conferences with the Soviets, he quickly defended the exchange of notes: better a thorough exchange of notes and then a short, successful conference than no exchange of notes followed by a long but abortive conference. In response to Friedländer's question whether a future all-German government would be obliged to support Western integration, Adenauer provided a de facto denial of the commitment clause in Article 7, Paragraph 3, of the Bonn Convention, even though the first, completely unambiguous version of this clause was already included in the draft agreement:

> The conclusion of the general agreement and the integration of the Federal Republic in the Western defense system in no way represents the closing of the "all-German door." The general agreement provides for the re-examination of all treaties in the event of German reunification. But the Federal Republic cannot now be expected to renounce her "European Policy" nor to commit an all-German Government before it has been formed, to such a renunciation. The ratification of the general agreement by the Parliaments does not, however, create faits accomplis in respect of an all-German state.

On the other hand, he continued, it would be wrong to believe that the objective of German reunification could be achieved by delaying the signature of the contract by a few weeks or months. If this were done, the Germans would find themselves falling between two stools. What mattered was not the timing of signature, but the goodwill in principle of the Russians. So long as they insisted on German neutrality or on the Oder–Neisse line as a frontier, such goodwill would not be apparent. The neutralization of Germany proposed by the Soviet note would render her helpless and destroy her freedom. The creation of a German national army would not alter matters since her present geographical circumstances made it impossible to defend German territory unaided. As for the "insinuations" that he—for either party, political, or religious reasons—did not regard the eighteen million Germans of the Soviet zone as an absolutely welcome addition to the Federal Republic, he said:

> Party politics and religion play no role at all here. I do not even wish to address the question whether the SPD would be the strongest party in free all-German elections. But this much I can say with great certainty: I would always prefer a Germany reunited in freedom in which the SPD was the strongest party to a Federal Republic separated from the Soviet zone but in which the CDU was the strongest party. In such a matter, the fatherland takes precedence over the party and the statesman certainly is not ruled by the party. Nor is the statesman ruled by religion. Moreover, I would be a poor Christian if I were to prefer to abandon the Germans in the Soviet zone to slavery because the majority of them are Protestants. In the all-German question, there is no CDU policy and no Catholic policy. Neither of these policies exist, just as an SPD policy or a Protestant policy on this issue could not exist.

In conclusion, he reiterated his fundamental position: German unity was closely bound up with peace in the world. If efforts to restore German unity should be unsuccessful, this would prove that the German question could not be solved in isolation. If reunification could be achieved at all at the present time, it would be achieved; if not, the matter would only be postponed. The power of the West was increasing and it was better to negotiate from strength; there were good reasons for having confidence.[9]

This interview, in particular Adenauer's indication that the treaties could be reevaluated in the event of reunification, generated excitement, especially in Paris. In fact, Adenauer's primary concern was to "take the wind out of the S.P.D. sails," as Kirkpatrick correctly recognized and as Adenauer succeeding in doing. If the letter had been published before this interview, the public would have had the impression that Adenauer was "bowing to SPD pressure." The SPD was furious about Adenauer's maneuvering and withdrew its offer to discuss things.[10]

More important than this, however, the SPD "was now apparently prepared to accept even the neutralization of an all-German state," Kurt Klotzbach noted, and "the real explosiveness of the Social Democratic commentary" lay precisely in its tolerating this condition.[11] In his *Erinnerungen*, Adenauer takes the occasion of Schumacher's letter to thoroughly condemn the SPD's "vacillations" and to again underscore the basic principles of his policy. He concludes: "We certainly could not trust the Russians. We had to choose. What the Russians wanted was clear; they wanted to use Germany's neutrality to draw Germany into the Soviet sphere of influence. What the West offered us was explicitly stated in the Bonn Convention and in the European Defense Community Treaty."[12]

In April and May 1952, the Western powers argued in exactly the same fashion. In view of German public opinion, they now wanted to pursue an offensive policy. On April 16, the U.S. State Department presented a strategy paper discussing how American propaganda should present the Soviet note. The aim was to help the Germans understand that integration into the Western alliance was the only proper course for them and that the path the Soviets proposed would result in the entire German nation's falling into servitude.

This strategy paper recalls Adenauer's memoirs, so similar are the arguments. It explored the question of what would happen if the Soviets' proposal for a united, democratic Germany were to be implemented and were to suggest to the Soviet Union that its offer had resulted in an independent, "neutral" Germany. Either the Soviet zone would continue to be occupied by Soviet troops, in which case neither independence nor freedom nor neutrality would result, or all the occupying troops would be withdrawn, leaving the Soviet troops on the Oder–Neisse border and the Western troops holding an uncertain bridgehead in France. This latter possibility would create a completely new situation in Europe whose effects on the policies of the NATO countries, including the United States, would be difficult to anticipate. Such a vacuum would virtually invite Eastern aggression and domination and would permit neither independence nor neutrality. Thus the inevitable conclusion was that as long as the Soviets do not change their way of thinking, "neutrality for Germany is impossible."

In view of the Soviet threat, the U.S. strategy paper argued, it must be the aim of every patriotic German to give precedence to a policy that would bring Germany protection and security. Therefore the close integration of a free Western Europe would contain every guarantee that the responsible German leadership was seeking in the national interest. Germany had everything to gain from the policy of European integration and was in an excellent position to be a leader in it. The building of Western strength through integration including Germany was entirely compatible with the achieving of German unity on livable terms, that is, under conditions of freedom, strength, and security. In conclusion, the Germans must not be allowed to picture themselves as facing the choice of integration or unity.[13]

The staff in the British Foreign Office agreed in principle with this paper, even though it was rather wordy and highly colored. However, there was an important difference of emphasis between their approach and the line proposed in the American paper. They had been careful not to give the Germans the impression that they were "slamming the door" on the Russian proposals, for there was no doubt that a large proportion of German opinion favored at least discussions with the Russians to find out "whether they mean business." Another element in the American directive also seemed "potentially dangerous": the view that the Federal Republic might be a "leader" in an integrated Western Europe. The Foreign Office expressed concern about emphasizing this view out of consideration for the French. This view was in keeping with a telegram from the American embassy in Paris that made yet another point: the French were not at all interested in German unity as such, and their qualms about the European Defense Community derived precisely from their fear that at the appropriate moment the Germans would maneuver the community into a war designed to recapture the lost territories.[14]

Even though the situation for the Western powers grew more difficult despite the "offensive strategy" and public opinion in France and Germany was so volatile and indeed hysterical, as Kirkpatrick reported to London, the Western powers' fundamental position remained constant. Until the European Defense Community Treaty and the Bonn Convention were signed, they wanted to continue to "play for time."[15] The response note was viewed as a "delaying tactic," which, in Eden's opinion, should be drafted in such a way as to "make an impact on the mind of the man in the street in the free world."[16] However, in order not to provoke unexpected reactions, the door to negotiations with the Soviet Union should not be slammed. And as Schuman had already remarked on April 19, the West should not appear to be running away from conversations either.[17]

Eight days earlier, after receiving the second Soviet note, Vincent Auriol, the French president, had given Antoine Pinay his assessment of the situation and had taken a position on the German problem. Auriol was convinced that Germany would never give up on its lost territories and its 1937 borders. The German military would take advantage of every means of overcoming the effects of their defeat, either by turning to Russia or—if that should come to nothing—by drawing the West into a war of conquest that would be passed off as a response to aggression. In view of these circumstances, Auriol stated:

> I believe as you do that we *cannot* adopt a *purely negative posture*. If we were only dealing with propaganda, as our American friends have sometimes maintained, it would be clever to respond with *constructive opposing propaganda* that would satisfy the demands of justice and enlighten the people.
>
> But I do not believe that it is only a question of propaganda. The Russians fear Germany, and they also worry that Germany will enter into alliances only in order to reconquer the Eastern territories. Thus, one must *exploit this fear* without relinquishing our means of defense. Therefore, I believe we must affirm that as long as no peace treaty exists for all of the powers who fought against Germany in the war, France will continue to pursue the formation of a European army and the development of an [organized] Europe including Germany; that nothing will cause us to depart from this course; and that it is up to the Russians to expand the European organization by joining it.
>
> On the other hand, I believe we must strongly agree to holding *free elections* in Germany, to preparing for these elections, and to verifying their fairness. But the commission charged with preparing and *overseeing* [the elections] need not necessarily be a United Nations commission. By mutual agreement, the four "great powers" could also select three powers to do this.
>
> Perhaps we could propose the following concerning the *German army*. In keeping with what has already been decided, Germany would be demilitarized and militarily neutralized, under the following conditions:
>
> Troops under United Nations control would be positioned on the left bank of the Rhine and along the eastern border. Here and there Germany could provide a contingent, whose size would be mutually agreed upon, in order to defend its military and political neutrality. Americans, some Belgians, Luxemburgians, and French could be po-

sitioned on the left bank of the Rhine with a German contingent, and Russians, Czechs, Norwegians, and Swedes on the other side, also with a German contingent. Thus, neutrality would be subjected to United Nations control, and Germany would be free to form alliances within the framework of the United Nations unless the Russians do not want to join an economically and politically organized Europe.

In reference to the *borders*, I would like to recall the *Potsdam* conference. Contrary to the Soviet interpretation, there is no question that the allies in Potsdam only pledged themselves to endorse certain Soviet proposals and that they postponed the final determination of borders, especially of Poland's borders, until a peace conference. One could readily respond: the peace conference will explore what possible border agreements can be reached between Germany and Russia, respectively German and the other nations in order to eliminate the seeds of conflict that would arise from irredentism. In addition, once Europe is definitively organized, nothing would justify the annexation of territory.

In conclusion, let me note that when I propose other possibilities for overseeing the elections apart from the United Nations commission, this is certainly not in order to defend the Russian assertion that *Article 107* excludes United Nations intervention in German affairs. Article 107 establishes that the charter does not prohibit a combined governmental action vis-à-vis Germany, but it does not in any way rule out United Nations intervention in the solution of the German problem.

In my view we are only dealing with a concession designed to attain a result. These are a few suggestions.[18]

The French government did not adopt Auriol's suggestions, nor did it stray from its already chosen path.

At this point, however, Washington began to play a more active role. According to the American view, the Soviets were playing a game of deceit. Their willingness to make any sort of concessions remained, even after the second note, "shrouded in mystery and this no doubt represents their intention at this stage of game," as the American ambassador in Paris reported to Washington.[19] On April 11 at the State Department, Philip C. Jessup wondered whether, in view of the increasing disquiet among the West German public, they should perhaps try "to force the Russians to decide as quickly as possible whether they would allow elections in their zone."[20] Apparently they had now reached the point where talks could no longer be prevented. On April 29, Acheson decided to follow the course outlined at the meeting on April 1: no talks at the foreign ministers' level but talks between the high commissioners or their representatives. However, these talks should in no way endanger the signing of the treaties. Now the strategy was to underscore the advantages of integration policy, while being careful to avoid creating the impression that the three Western powers had formulated this policy and were now insisting on its implementation. Instead, it should be emphasized that this was the policy of the Federal Republic and other European countries that the United States and Great Britain were *supporting*. And then came the decisive sentence: "[I] believe this point important as many Germans tend to feel we are forcing Germany down path of *our* choosing." Since some sort of talks were probably necessary, it is now desirable "to take the initiative in proposing them in order to convince Germans we mean business and are not afraid to talk, and to control level, substance and timing of talk. Department has come increasingly to conclusion in this regard that we have much to gain and nothing to lose by making specific proposal in this reply for talks."

Even though Acheson was convinced that the object of these talks was to "expose Soviet insincerity at earliest possible date," his objective in holding talks with the Soviets had remained at the center of the controversy about both the failure to explore the Soviet note and the Soviets' "true intentions." Acheson continued: "If Soviets are really prepared to open Eastern Zone, we should force their hand. We can *not* allow our plans to be thwarted merely by *speculation* that Soviets may be ready actually to pay a high price."[21]

Here was yet another opportunity to do what Schumacher had demanded on April 22: to ascertain whether Germany could be reunified under conditions of freedom and, in any case, to make it clear that the Federal Republic had not failed to explore all the proffered chances for German reunification and for peace in Europe. Since none other than the American secretary of state made such an offer—even if only for tactical reasons—then certainly the frequently cited danger of "sitting between two chairs" did not exist for the Germans, nor did the ultimatum: "With the West or with the East." And Adenauer? Was he again "more American than the Americans" as Jakob Kaiser had accused him of being in March?

On the afternoon of May 2, McCloy informed Adenauer of the State Department's proposal. Initially, Adenauer did not reject this suggestion.[22] But his final decision had an entirely different look. That this decision was not easy for him to make is evidenced by his requiring an entire day and half the night to evaluate the alternatives. Then he informed McCloy that he opposed negotiations. McCloy cabled Dean Acheson on May 3, 1952:

> Chancellor told me today that after serious consideration yesterday and "through half the night," he has definitely concluded US proposal for meeting in Berlin (paragraph 9 Department's telegram 2850) would be a mistake at this time. If meeting is now (repeat now) suggested, Chancellor doubts that Cabinet would authorize him to sign contractual agreements until meeting had demonstrated whether Soviets sincere in their offer of free elections. He would expect opposition to insist that meetings take place before signature, but now (repeat now) fears even members of Government would take same line. He also believes it would be unwise to limit any quadripartite meeting to discussion of free election issue as Soviets might be prepared to make sufficient concessions to justify lengthy negotiations. During course of these, public attention would be concentrated on the concessions and tend to overlook other objectionable phases of Soviet proposal. In these circumstances it would be impossible to conclude defence negotiations.[23]

Adenauer's historic decision to reject negotiations severely burdened his own policy. In his *Erinnerungen*, he failed to mention this American offer at all, and this was plainly not an oversight. That he was conscious of the magnitude of his decision is nowhere so clear as in the chapter concerning the "Russian note offensive." One is reminded of Bismarck when Adenauer writes: "In politics, ideal circumstances will probably never occur. If they do occur, they mark great moments in history. However, the questions then arise: are there also statesmen present who recognize these circumstances, and will their people follow them?"[24] Looking back after fourteen years, after the failure of his policy was evident even to him, did Adenauer want to indicate that one of these great moments in history had appeared in the spring of 1952 — as it had in the spring of 1955 for Austria — and that the German people were not ready or "mature" enough for a different decision to have been made? The decisiveness with which Adenauer answered his self-posed question and defended his policy certainly permits such an interpretation.

If Adenauer had accepted the American offer, then the Foreign Office and the Quai d'Orsay — where Acheson's proposal encountered opposition — would also have had to agree. Even McCloy was not especially enthusiastic, and Kirkpatrick argued as Adenauer did: the political parties in the Federal Republic would propose stalling tactics and would force Adenauer to postpone the signing. Thus the entire schedule would be ruined.[25] As the deputy French high commissioner stated on May 2 about the offer, the Soviets "would accept it and talks would begin; once begun, they would be hard to stop. Time would slip by and the whole now-or-never project of European integration would founder." In any case, a mere discussion between representatives of the high commissioners would not convince the French and German public that a serious and exhaustive exploration of the Soviet position had been made. Then talks at a higher level would be needed. These talks could take place, but not too soon. Further notes would first be needed "to expose Soviet insincerity and fix firmer foundations for an eventual encounter."[26]

After the second Soviet note, free elections, which had been the hope of the opposition, were definitely no longer the decisive issue. Even assuming that there would be massive vote fraud in the GDR and that all East Germans would vote for the SED, the Communists would still have remained in a hopeless minority in the National Assembly. Neither was the issue any longer that of ascertaining whether the Soviet offer would permit Germany to participate in the Schuman Plan. Adenauer was certain from the beginning that this would not be possible, although, interestingly enough, the concrete question was never put to the Soviet government.

This question appeared in the British draft of the response on April 21, but not in the actual note of May 13. The reasons are apparent. More was at stake, as the French foreign minister made clear in a personal memorandum to his British colleague on May 6. According to Schuman, Germany, as had already happened so often in its history, found itself faced with the problem of its unity, a problem with which it was obsessed and which the Russians had been able to make the prize of a supreme temptation: to achieve immediate unification in return for certain postponements and certain questionable conditions. The Russian maneuver was more successful than expected, as the confusion everywhere indicated. In Schuman's view, the West had perhaps depended too exclusively on the safeguard that they had in the incontestable sincerity and the personal authority of Adenauer. However, it had now been shown that neither one nor the other had been sufficient to prevent a profound disquiet breaking out in the ranks of his coalition and even of his own party. German public opinion was wondering which road it should follow:

The moment has finally come for the Germans to acknowledge that the unity being offered them contains important unknown elements and certain servitude.

The Russian tempter knew how to focus everyone's attention on the freedom of all-German elections. Certainly this is an important problem; but it is definitely not insurmountable. And I presume that the Russians would risk everything to hold the elections if they could attain a German central government for this price, since this would mean the end of the Federal Republic, enemy number 1.

How can we effectively counteract this? With sophistry that makes the elections impossible? We would lose this game with the Germans. Moreover, this is not the actual problem at all.

The procedure by which unity is created is less important than defining this unity itself. Even the fanatical Germans and those most enamored of unity must recognize that unity is not everything, that unity in servitude—that is, unity subject to some kind of Russian control—might temporarily give East Germany a reprieve, but would mean a large step backward and renewed surrender for Germany as a whole.

This is the truth we must expressly convey to everyone. We must bring the Russians to the point where they themselves begin to demonstrate this. By demanding clarifications, we will put an end to the silence that has so far obscured their contradictions. We must ultimately know what regime would govern a united Germany, [a Germany] united but occupied by the four powers and from whom any sort of treaty would be withheld.

To form a central government without previously guaranteeing this government a minimum of freedom to negotiate would mean paralyzing Germany and placing it at the mercy of Soviet maneuvers. We understand this; Germany will also understand this if we know how to explain and disseminate [this truth].

Insistently posing these questions will be in Germany's as well as in our own interest. We will then transfer the debate to the proper ground: the weaknesses of our adversary. We will reveal that everything that glitters is not gold. The actual intentions of all parties will be disclosed. At the same time, our relations with Germany will be placed on a healthier footing. We will successfully overcome the prevailing reserve and mistrust. We will no longer adopt the position of those who plead for unity for tactical reasons while hoping that it will not occur. In the past, it seemed that our egotistical concerns would prevent an honest search for common goals. On the other hand, we will stop allowing ourselves to be dangerously outbid for there is a risk that Germany will make us pay much too high a price if the negotiations are indefinitely disputed or protracted.

Germany must be made to bear the entire burden of its own responsibility. Germany will have to choose not between Western integration and unity, for this would be an impossible dilemma, but between unity with guarantees of liberty such as we have offered and unity under four-power control.

In short, Germany must be convinced that it is in its own interest to stand with us even in the quest for unity.[27]

In Schuman's opinion, the greatest danger was that the Germans could be tempted to seek unity at any price. The West's slogan therefore should not be just "free elections," but "free elections for a free Germany." Schuman felt, as Etienne de Crouy-Chanel emphasized on May 7 to the American ambassador in London, that the West must take the initiative to show the Germans that the choice was not really between Europe or unity but between "unity with liberty or unity with slavery." If the West could show them this, the Germans would be far more ready to choose the West. The Germans now thought the West was less interested in the unity issue than in integration with the West, but "we must demonstrate that we are ready now for a reunited Germany on the sole condition that it is a free Germany. We cannot escape the dilemma which the Soviets have put us and the Germans in if we concentrate only on a unified Germany. Only if we give equal emphasis to freedom for the united Germany can we demonstrate to the Germans that they have no chance for freedom unless they join our side." The Soviets had refused to say anything about the position of the German government before the peace treaty, which they would be in a position easily to postpone indefinitely. Here was a chance for the West, Schuman felt: "We must smoke them out on this issue."[28]

Would a neutral unified Germany have become communist or have fallen under Soviet control? Both at the time and in retrospect, Adenauer responded with a decisive yes. Even in his memoirs he categorically asserted that "neutralization means Sovietization."[29] And presumably, this is what Stalin hoped. In the West, public warnings against such a development were frequent.

In fact, however, even at the time, confidential analyses revealed a different view. A secret U.S. State Department report from May 14, 1952, for example, investigated what would probably happen in (West) Germany, Western Europe, and the Soviet Union if the West were to reject (or, respectively, accept) a bona fide Soviet proposal (the existing offer was not considered bona fide) for the formation of a Germany reunified (but without the territories east of the Oder–Neisse rivers), neutralized, and armed in a limited fashion.

The answer is instructive: a communist Germany was not foreseen; expected instead was a "moderate and democratic" all-German government that, although relatively pro-Western in its orientation, would follow "a basically neutral foreign policy." Even if the economic situation were to worsen, the possibility of a communist regime was not considered likely. By contrast, a rightist, authoritarian regime was considered a possibility, one that would pursue an opportunistic foreign policy but that "would not involve any acceptance of Kremlin control." However, it was feared that a neutralized Germany would have extensive consequences for Western Europe. Within Western Europe, this development would be interpreted as a sign of detente; this would reduce the willingness to carry out large-scale military programs in most countries, with the exception of France, which would wish to rearm to keep pace with the remilitarization of a united Germany. Meanwhile, the Kremlin would continue the cold war, placing special emphasis on attempts to subvert or seduce Germany.

On the other hand, rejecting such an offer would probably lead to a serious reaction among the West German population. The people would be so embittered that it would be virtually impossible for any West German government to carry forward rearmament and "unification-Westward" policies effectively. In Western Europe the view that the United States was leading the Western coalition toward war would be strengthened; neutralist and anti-American sentiment would grow. In France, as elsewhere in Western Europe, popular support for rearmament would decline.[30]

Hard work and great rhetorical skill were needed before the Western editorial committee in London could agree on the response note which was delivered in Moscow on May 13.[31] The goal was to postpone a conference for months and then to limit its agenda to the issues of the elections and the formation of a government: "The Soviets were to relinquish the GDR without knowing what conditions they would be able to impose on a reunified Germany in the interests of their security," as the West German political scientist, Richard Löwenthal, put it.[32]

The *actual* Western response was in fact the signing of the Bonn Convention in Bonn on May 26 and of the European Defense Community Treaty in Paris on the following day. The Bonn Convention was signed in the same hall in which the Basic Law had been adopted three years earlier. Initially, Acheson opposed signing the treaties in Bonn, since he feared that nationalist forces in Germany could later take advantage of this. He favored Strassburg and was only prepared to come to Bonn for a day or two thereafter if this would "gild the pill" for Adenauer. He next proposed The Hague as the "ideal place, prominently associated as it is with the ideals of peace and containing the Peace Palace." But in the end, he agreed to sign the document in Bonn. Bonn was Adenauer's choice, and Adenauer was supported by the British, who wanted to help the prestige of Adenauer and the federal government by a ceremony at Bonn, "which badly needs some such glamour."[33]

Adenauer viewed the signing of the treaties as the "crowning achievement of his political career; he looked forward to the moment when they were to be signed and wanted to celebrate it in a festive way and to keep the days on which the treaties were signed in Bonn and Paris as holidays in the people's memory."[34] As Baring reported, Undersecretary Lenz convinced Adenauer to celebrate the event with a torchlight procession, an indispensable element in the age of mass psychology. Minister of the Interior Lehr requested that the state governments display flags on public buildings, declare a school holiday, and point out the importance of the treaties to children.[35]

But this was too much and nothing came of it all. Schumacher's judgment remained: "One cannot achieve German unity with a policy of strength and with military power. This only shows that one does not truly want it. . . . Whoever approves this treaty ceases to be a good German."[36]

How should one celebrate a treaty whose precise contents were not even known? And SPD Bundestag member Adolf Arndt's comment that a previous torchlight procession had resulted in all of Germany burning was certainly relevant as well.[37]

On the same day the Bonn Convention was signed, the GDR government announced that the demarcation line would be cordoned off. Thereafter the border was marked by a five-kilometer-wide prohibited zone and a ten-meter-wide control strip that became a death strip for many people. Nothing could have better documented the division of Germany.

A further turning point came a few weeks later, at the second SED party congress from July 9 to 12, 1952. Apparently this was what the U.S. High Commission had predicted since early June: the Soviet Union would tighten its grip on the GDR and transform it into a complete satellite state. Possibly, however, the SED also wanted to influence developments and, from the outset, pull the rug out from under any future considerations of German unity. The question remains to what extent the "construction of the foundation of socialism" now proclaimed by the SED would not have been a topic for the party congress before the treaties with the West were signed. In any event, SED General Secretary Walter Ulbricht now announced: "The democratic and economic development as well as the consciousness of the working class and of the majority of working people are now so well developed that the construction of socialism has become a fundamental task."[38]

This announcement marked the second phase of the revolutionary process of change: complete centralization of bureaucracy, strict subjugation of the state machinery to the authority of the SED, restructuring of the system of justice, formation of a national armed forces, complete nationalization of industry, and partial collectivization of agriculture.

CHAPTER EIGHT

THE END OF THE BATTLE OF THE NOTES

With Adenauer's Help, a Victory for the Western Powers

On May 24, the Soviet government presented its response[1] to the Western note from May 13. Apparently the Kremlin had realized that Western policy was a fait accompli. Even the tone of this note differed considerably from that of the first two notes; the choice of words recalled well-known Soviet propaganda, and the reference to four-power responsibilities prescribed by the Potsdam agreement was not especially attractive even to Adenauer's critics. This note was "put together hurriedly," the British ambassador in Moscow stated, at the "eleventh hour," just before the treaties with the West were signed.[2] His American colleague Kennan expressed it even more explicitly: "This note is not the authentic, terse, collected, menacing voice of Stalin's Kremlin when functioning in high gear and pursuing an important Soviet initiative"; instead it appeared that this extraordinarily weak opus was the work of low-ranking "hacks supplied only with grudging, cryptic and guarded instructions and told to make best of it."[3]

Acheson told Eden that Adenauer did not regard this note as in any way dangerous to him and that it would indeed make this task easier.[4] In Bonn the reaction to this note was nearly unanimous. Heinrich Krone believed that it was a move designed to cloak the Soviets' embarrassment regarding Germany. He called the note "extremely clumsy" since it deprived the SPD and the German Federation of Trade Unions (DGB) of an important part of their arguments against Adenauer's policy.[5] For Hermann Schäfer, the FDP leader in the Bundestag, this was the final demonstration that the Soviets were not sincere. The West should now place the blame for Germany's continued division squarely on the Soviet Union. If talks were to be held at all, then only after ratification of the treaties. Hans Mühlenfeld of the German Party favored a quick response in order "to unmask Soviet insincerity and to rob [the] SPD of [a] potentially powerful argument," as McCloy's deputy, Samuel Reber, reported to Washington. Franz Josef Strauss from the CSU held a similar view, but in a radio interview on May 28, Adenauer again argued for four-power talks, if they seemed to promise success. Reber dismissed this as lip service, which it probably was.

Only Jakob Kaiser, whom McCloy characterized as the leader of a very small "starry-eyed minority" in the CDU, told the U.S. high commissioner that the situation had not been changed, that the door to negotiations stood as open as ever. But Franz Thedieck, Kaiser's undersecretary, who saw things more realistically, reassured the U.S. high commissioner that only an extreme optimist could still hold this view. He considered the note clumsy and ill-advised: "Back to Potsdam is not good enough," he stated. The judgment of the Russian expert in the German Foreign Ministry, Hans von Herwarth, was similar. In his view, the note was the "dumbest he had ever read and had greatly assisted Adenauer." He believed that the style and tone of the note indicated that Stalin himself had probably not even read it and that it probably meant that the Kremlin had now realized that its first note was "too little and too late" to win the Germans over to their side.[6] The West had won the "battle of the notes" against the Soviets, as Foreign Minister Eden contentedly reassured Acheson and Schuman in Paris on May 28.[7]

In this connection—and especially in view of the note from March 10—the concluding analysis of the U.S. High Commission in Bonn dated June 2 offers some interesting information. According to this document, the American High Commission was inclined to believe that the first Soviet note was serious and contained the terms for a peace treaty. The very harshness of these terms gave the note a ring of authenticity, a "take it or leave it tone." With this note, the Kremlin had bluntly indicated the basis on which it would "then, now and in indefinite future" settle the German question by mutual agreement with the West. Although these terms were obviously unacceptable to the West, the Kremlin might have hoped to confuse the population in the Federal Republic and "undo our grand design for Europe." The Soviets had not succeeded, but it remained to be seen which maneuver they would choose next.

However, at this juncture, the Soviets had evidently decided to strengthen their grip on the Eastern zone and to harden it into a thoroughgoing satellite, thus aggravating East–West tensions rather than alleviating them. But—"and this is an important but"—in everything that the Kremlin did, it had been careful to appear to leave the door open to negotiate a solution of the German problem. In the opinion of the High Commission, this was the decisive factor in interpreting the last Soviet note, which had been more than a notebook for propaganda designed to undermine support for Western integration. The Soviets also wanted to document that they were the ones seeking a solution to the German question. Even if it appeared that the West had been victorious, those in the West must continue to remain vigilant, for it could not be assumed that the Kremlin "is sobered and incapable of desperate action of one who imagines hostile force slowly closing in on him." Thus, in responding to the note, the West (1) must not appear to shut the door on negotiations and (2) must keep to the forefront the main issue that it is "we who seek peaceful solution of German problem."[8]

Remarkably, the Western powers required seven weeks to respond to the Soviet note. Thus, bizarrely, the Western response was delivered only after the United States Senate had already ratified the Western treaties. What was the reason for this delay?

Even though the West had won the battle of the notes, the Soviets were obviously going to spare no effort to prevent the treaties from being ratified. For this reason, the Western powers agreed to continue corresponding with the Soviets, to refer to the proposals already made in the Western note of May 13 (Points 2 to 4: independent commission), and to declare their readiness to participate in a relatively low-level meeting on receipt of the Soviet note. This time around, the U.S. State Department was to work up a first draft of the response.

This draft was ready a few days later, but now Foreign Minister Schuman went a decisive step further. He wanted, without further hesitation, to invite the Soviet Union to a four-power conference, first at the level of ambassadors, then at the level of foreign ministers. He did not want to await the report of the commission regarding conditions for holding elections in Germany, for, in any case, the composition of this commission had yet to be agreed upon. Instead, the conditions for holding immediate free elections throughout Germany should be examined at the conclusion of this conference. In addition, an all-German "statute" should be devised that would guarantee an all-German government formed on the basis of free elections the freedom to negotiate until peace treaties were concluded and that would prevent the return of four-power control. Moreover, he proposed in very general terms that the problems connected with reunification and a peace treaty be discussed. As Schuman told the British ambassador, he had come to the conclusion that the Soviets were "completely at a loss"; they did not know where to go. The West, on the other hand, were in a strong position and should now "take the initiative."[9]

The American ambassador in Paris, James Clement Dunn, gave four reasons for Schuman's surprising offer:

1. French discomfort with continued West German rearmament. This led to their constantly clutching at straws in the hope of reaching an agreement with the Russians.

2. The demand for negotiations made at the party congress of the Popular Republican Movement and by the radicals.

3. Schuman's conviction that the West's position would be strengthened by signing the European Defense Community Treaty and the Bonn Convention.

4. His conviction that following another failed attempt to hold four-power talks, ratification of the treaties would be more readily accepted in France.[10]

The French initiative generated considerable irritation in Washington, and great efforts were needed to dissuade Schuman from his plan. As Philip Jessup stressed to Acheson, everything should be done by all three governments "to minimize the impression of a split since such an impression could assist nobody but the Soviets."[11]

In the meantime, Eden had also considered further tactics, and now he, too, advocated a meeting with the Soviets, since, once the European Defense Community Treaty was signed there was no longer any reason to fear such a meeting. In his opinion, by proposing such a meeting Western leaders should be able to consolidate Western opinion behind their policy and thus improve the prospects for ratifying the treaties, more especially in France and in the Federal Republic. Nevertheless, he felt a decisive limitation should be made: this conference should not broach the subject of a peace treaty before an all-German government had been formed to take part in the discussion but must confine itself to debating the proposals made on May 13.

Acheson strongly opposed this proposal. In his opinion, the Soviets would construe such an invitation as a weakness. In Germany, no demand at all existed for such a conference; thus the public's view of Western policy would be confused rather than strengthened. Although Paris had, in the meantime, accepted the British view that a peace treaty should not be discussed, Acheson's objections remained: the U.S. Senators would be confused and would not ratify the treaties until such a four-power conference were concluded. Adenauer was also opposed to four-power talks. The French proposal could be of benefit to no one, "except our enemies." We must focus on those issues that the Russians have not yet responded to. Therefore, the West should emphatically insist on its prerequisites for conducting free elections. Acheson's concern revolved primarily around Adenauer. The British ambassador described Acheson's view in a telegram on June 19: "Adenauer had asked us for time to help him obtain ratification, and if we failed him, and ratification in Germany was seriously delayed, or even rendered impossible, we would have destroyed our work of the last 18 months. This was a risk which he would not take." Adenauer thought the West "ought to hammer away at the conditions for free elections."[12]

Again it was the British, together with the American ambassador in London, who found a compromise that was finally accepted by all sides after some troublesome arguments. The most difficult problem was satisfying Adenauer's wishes. When the treaties were signed with the West, the situation changed fundamentally in his eyes. Even though the treaties were not yet ratified, Adenauer now saw himself as an equal partner with the right to exercise a formative influence on policy. Gone were the days in which he was only informed and in which he offered the high commissioners unbinding recommendations for their consideration. In his *Erinnerungen,* Adenauer thoroughly explores the "sharp disagreements" with the high commissioners.[13] He now presented himself as the one making the demands and submitting the proposals for changes. On the evening of July 2, Federal Republic Undersecretary Hallstein even let members of the high commission come to him when he needed to give them a memorandum; previously it had always been the other way around. In rejecting four-power negotiations, Adenauer and McCloy became allies against the French.

On June 25, when Adenauer was informed of the intended response to the Soviet note, which did not exclude talks with the Soviets, he reacted brusquely, and the conversation went "rather badly." He rejected any talks with the Soviets before the treaties were ratified and demanded a response that was both "as hard and as rough as possible."[14] He insistently stressed that he was not very impressed by the theory that another four-power conference was necessary in order to convince the public of the Soviets' true intentions. Holding another unsuccessful conference would not convince those who were still not satisfied. The majority that, he claimed, existed in the Bundestag and in the population for his policy did not need this demonstration, although it might be necessary in France. He then interjected a highly unusual argument: the refugees who had recently come from the Soviet zone were strongly against a further conference with the Russians, which they regarded as completely useless.[15]

On the British side, a different view prevailed. They did not want to shut the door on talks with the Soviets and wanted to stick to the main lines of the last note despite Adenauer's views, which, they thought, "almost certainly fail to reflect majority German opinion." Should four-power talks occur, contrary to all expectations, they wanted to reassure Adenauer that "there will be no question of our coming to a secret agreement with the Russians behind Germany's back."[16] This was exactly what Adenauer feared: the four powers would work out a peace treaty and would then present this to an all-German government. In his view, this would be a direct refutation of Article 7 of the Bonn Convention, which stated that the Federal Republic and the three powers agreed "that an essential aim of their common policy is a peace settlement of the whole of Germany, freely negotiated between Germany and her former enemies."[17]

On July 2, Adenauer gave the high commissioners his proposals for changes in the response note.[18] For the British Deputy High Commissioner John Guthrie Ward, Adenauer's argument that "the draft reply implies readiness on the allies part to work out a draft peace treaty with the Soviet Government behind the back of the future all-German Government" was "typically subtle and suspicious." As a result, the high commissioners met with Adenauer for four hours on July 3 in an encounter characterized by sharp disagreement. Their attempt to dispel Adenauer's mistrust failed miserably, for, as Ward reported to London, "nothing of course would really satisfy him, except a radical change of course, which I realise is out of the question," especially since the French cabinet had already approved the draft of the response note. But, as Ward stated in his closing appraisal, "maddening though his attitude is, it is in our interest to save his face at this time."[19] On the same day, Adenauer delivered an aide-mémoire in which he stated his desire for change more precisely, and in an accompanying memorandum to McCloy, he clarified his concerns.[20]

Adenauer's mistrust was unfounded in this case. In fact, the Western allies did not intend to double-cross the chancellor as he feared. Thus, the British and the Americans considered it both possible and desirable to provide him with the reassurances he desired. The French grudgingly agreed. But when Adenauer then requested that the note not be delivered in Moscow before the Western treaties were first read in the Bundestag on July 9 and 10, the patience of the French came to an end. François-Poncet believed it was time for the allies to teach Adenauer "a sharp lesson by cutting short their deference to Adenauer's views in this matter."[21]

Paris refused to meet with Adenauer again. They did not want the French public to be able to accuse them of becoming Adenauer's "lackeys."[22] Nevertheless, the British and Americans fulfilled Adenauer's wish, without informing the French in advance. On the evening before the Bundestag debate, they gave Adenauer the final text of the note, which now corresponded to his requests. As Ward reported to London, Adenauer was "apparently very pleased with our efforts to meet him."[23]

The formulation that was finally agreed upon went as follows: "There should be an early meeting of representatives of the four Governments, provided it is understood that the four Governments are in favor of free elections throughout Germany as described in paragraph 4 of the present note, and of the participation of a free German Government in the negotiation of a German peace treaty." Paragraph 4 went to the heart of the matter: free elections could be held only when the necessary preconditions existed throughout Germany.[24] This formulation allowed the West to determine whether the Soviet Union had fulfilled these preconditions; if so, then the only remaining concern was the composition and duties of the investigative commission. The issue of the "status" of an all-German government prior to a peace treaty was no longer mentioned.

Adenauer was very pleased about the Western response. Foreign Minister Vyshinskii was less so. When he received the note on July 10, his first impressions were evidently unfavorable. He complained that there were several misstatements in it concerning the Soviet policy toward Germany. When the British ambassador pursued this point, Vyshinskii replied that he must first carefully examine the note.[25] On August 23, the Soviet government responded. A large part of their response was devoted to attacking NATO, the European Defense Community Treaty, and the Bonn Convention. The issue of free elections was forced into the background. Instead, the Soviet note suggested that a commission composed of representatives from the Bundestag and the People's Chamber verify whether the necessary conditions existed for holding general free elections in Germany. At a four-power conference that was to take place in October at the latest, free elections were to be Point 3 on the agenda. Point 1 was to be preparation of a peace treaty with Germany; Point 2, the formation of an all-German government. In addition, the question of a date for withdrawing the occupying troops was to be discussed. Representatives of the GDR and the Federal Republic were to participate in this conference.[26]

In the U.S. State Department's view, all this was merely a "re-hash of old themes" aimed to create confusion and trouble in the Federal Republic. In the opinion of the British ambassador in Moscow, all indications pointed to the Soviets' having ruled out reunification and having decided to ardently pursue the integration of the GDR into the communist camp.[27] As in Washington, people in London and Paris were now also convinced that the Soviets had accepted the situation resulting from the treaties with the West having been signed, that they did not want to hold a four-power conference, that they were not interested in a democratic, free, reunified Germany in the Western sense—which was in itself no surprise—and instead that they had decided to proceed with "consolidating their hold on East Germany."[28] But the American embassy in Paris warned that it was premature and dangerous to act on the assumption that the Russians had abandoned the hope of preventing ratification or had played their last card: "We are not yet out of the wood."[29]

Operating on the basis of these beliefs, the Western powers responded to the Soviet note on September 23, even though Washington at first wanted to drop the exchange of notes.[30] The door to negotiations with the Soviets should not be shut—even Adenauer argued strongly for this. But one thing was very clear: negotiations would be conducted only on the basis of Western conditions. And these conditions read not only "free elections," but "free elections for a free Germany," a Germany free enough to become a member of the Western system of alliances. But this was merely a reaffirmation of the position held in the spring, as Soviet reactions indicated. The British ambassador reported to London: "To judge by the wry faces which [Deputy Foreign Minister] Pushkin pulled while the note was being read to him, I can only believe that its contents were not palatable to him, and that the shafts contained therein went home."[31]

The Soviet government did not reply to this note, thus ending the exchange. This neither surprised nor dismayed anyone in the West. After the European Defense Community Treaty and the Bonn Convention were signed, the Western notes were, at any rate, merely a compulsory exercise undertaken in deference to public opinion in France and in the Federal Republic. As early as August, George F. Kennan, the American ambassador to Moscow who was declared persona non grata by the Kremlin a short while later and expelled from the Soviet Union, expressed his intense criticism of the note diplomacy.

Kennan did not believe that anything could be gained by the exchange of notes, for it was too complicated and required too many compromises. The entire undertaking was not very convincing, would not lead to an agreement, and would not force the Soviets to change their behavior. Kennan even doubted the propaganda effect. At most, one might have gained some time, but at the price of exhausting the public's patience and encouraging apathy and cynicism about such diplomatic exchanges generally. As already mentioned, Adenauer persisted, even in his *Erinnerungen,* in characterizing the Soviets' refusal to grant the United Nations commission permission to enter East Germany to investigate whether conditions for free elections existed as "decisive" for judging the Soviet Union's serious intent. Kennan described his response to this position in a telegram to Acheson: it gave the impression of "archness and insincerity"; everyone knew that such conditions did not and could not possibly exist, and no United Nations commission was needed to prove that. Kennan's suggestion for proceeding ran as follows: stop the ostentatious exchange of notes and attempt to engage the Soviets in confidential talks concerning the German question on an oral diplomatic level to find out what sort of compromise, if any, the Soviets would be willing to make on the German problem. He explicitly emphasized his awareness of the difficulties and dangers in view of the still unratified treaties with the West. But sooner or later, they would need to talk to the Soviets, although this, of course, assumed that the Western powers really wanted German reunification and knew what price they were willing to pay for it.

In the margin of this passage in the telegram, Acheson wrote "later."[32]

The answer to Kennan's concerns was that the West wanted to continue the exchange of notes, while also exploring other possible diplomatic approaches to resolving the German question. The two should go hand in hand.[33]

But these other approaches were never to be explored.

CHAPTER NINE

THE STALIN NOTE:
A MISSED OPPORTUNITY

In conclusion, it can be said that, given everything we know about Soviet policy, Stalin's offer was serious; in 1952 a chance apparently existed for reunification. However, neither the Western powers nor Adenauer were interested in this goal; they had other goals in mind. Coming only seven years after the end of the war, the Soviet offer was amazingly far-reaching: a united, nonaligned Germany, with its own national army, its own armament production, the withdrawal of the occupying troops, no limitations on its nonmilitary economy, unrestricted participation by political parties, and the rehabilitation of former members of the armed forces. This offer is understandable only in light of the particularly "menacing circumstances" existing in the spring of 1952. And the seeming permanence of the Oder–Neisse line does not detract from the generosity of this offer, especially since it is unclear whether the Soviets ever gave their final word on the matter. The West's response to this offer was "stones instead of bread," as the

Soviet ambassador to Bonn, V. Semenov told his German colleague in Moscow, H. Groepper.[1]

Stalin made his offer at a historically unique moment that was never to recur. In reply to Graml's argument that the Soviet Union "throughout 1952 never offered reunification under acceptable conditions, namely by offering to sacrifice SED control by holding free, all-German elections," we must first mention that the simple equation between "acceptable" and "sacrificing SED control" does not accurately reflect the prevailing state of affairs. True, the Soviet Union did not offer precisely this. But to expect them to do so was naive, since the result of this offer might have been the advance of NATO troops up to the Oder. And that was exactly what the Soviets wanted to avoid. The price they were willing to pay for abandoning SED control was a nonaligned Germany.

Nor can we concede the validity of the "alibi thesis," that the Soviets' goal of firmly anchoring the GDR within the Eastern bloc was to be justified by blaming the West. The Soviet Union's decision to tighten its grip on the GDR and transform it into a complete satellite, as the American High Commission predicted on June 2, occurred more as a *reaction* to the rejection of the Soviet offer, if, in fact, the decision made by the second SED Party Conference concerning the "construction of socialism" is at all attributable to Soviet pressure.

Even the thesis that the Soviet Union wanted to "assist Western opponents of West European integration" cannot be sustained. On the contrary, by offering Germany its own national army, the Soviets practically pulled the rug out from beneath the feet of the Westerners opposed to integration. Moreover, Graml contradicts his own argument here by accurately pointing out in the same breath that the exchange of notes "significantly increased the willingness to sign the European Defense Community Treaty, especially in France."[2]

Since, after their initial hesitancy, the Western powers also believed that the note was serious, their reactions are especially interesting. They were not prepared to accept this "very dangerous" solution to the German question; they did not want a neutralized, unified Germany. For them, the risks and disadvantages of this arrangement were simply too great.

In the West, the fear of a reunified Germany was considerable. They worried that this Germany would revert to the seesaw policy it had pursued between the two world wars, would play off the East against the West, and, in the end, would decide in favor of the Soviet Union, since, with the territories east of the Oder and Neisse rivers, the Soviets had more to offer than the West did. The Rapallo complex was deeply rooted. Nowhere is the real issue more clearly stated than in the remark made by the acting British Foreign Minister, Lord Salisbury, to Churchill in 1953. With the European Defense Community Treaty and the Bonn Convention, one had prevented "so far as is humanly possible, a Soviet–German alignment"; this was "the main purpose" of the treaties.[3] In other words, the true issue was *control* of West Germany, not reunification. If no ideal German policy existed, then the path with the fewest risks must be chosen, and that was integrating the Federal Republic into the West.

The existing division of the country favored this solution, which was pushed enthusiastically in the spring of 1952 in order to create a fait accompli—thus the demand for both free elections *and* freedom for an all-German government to negotiate. This combination sounded "fair" but was later described as illusory, as almost "utopian," even among those in the West.[4] Stalin might possibly have discussed the first point, but the second was unacceptable and the West knew it. For this would have made it possible for a united Germany to do what Stalin hoped to prevent West Germany alone from doing: militarily integrating itself into the Western alliance. Thus the positions of East and West were irreconcilable from the beginning.

For Adenauer, reunification had only secondary importance. He excluded the alternative of Western integration or "unity in freedom." Instead, trusting the West implicitly, he viewed the first demand as a prerequisite for the second, made this position the publicly justified basis of his policy, and behaved accordingly. Thus, the Western powers had no reason to deviate from their position, although they unquestionably recognized the problem of counterposing Western integration and reunification and were themselves not fooled by their own propaganda depicting Western integration as the best route to independence. Without Adenauer's unconditional support, this course would scarcely have been sustainable. As early as November 1950, British High Commissioner Kirkpatrick described Adenauer as the best chancellor that they could hope for in terms of implementing the West's policy, despite whatever complaints they might have about him. Adenauer was exactly what he should not have been in the opinion of many and what Kaiser cautioned against in the cabinet meeting on March 11: "more American than the Americans."

If Stalin's offer had been a bluff, as was suggested to the West German public and as the majority of Adenauer's apologists still maintain today (although Adenauer himself probably believed this less than anyone), then the question remains why nobody forced Stalin to put his cards on the table, as the British diplomats Allen and Roberts suggested (see chapter 4) or as the Policy Planning Staff of the American State Department proposed. Nobody even posed the question of the Schuman Plan.

The West's attitude is the answer. For them, the entire "battle of the notes" was only a tactic: they opened a secondary theater of war, so to speak, with the goal of securing the German public's support for speedy Western integration.

As far as Adenauer's influence is concerned, Grewe himself states "that the moment the chancellor would have adopted a more positive attitude to the Soviet proposal, rather than responding as he did, his political importance would have become apparent in a very obvious fashion."[5] This is exactly the point, and to this extent it cannot be denied that the chance for reunification was bungled especially because of Adenauer's views on the matter. And despite Graml's claim, the American documents offer nothing to refute this position. That no attempt was even made to "explore" through direct negotiations just how far Stalin was really prepared to go remains Adenauer's historic responsibility of the spring of 1952. This is all the more inexplicable since several starting points existed for such exploration. After examining the documents, there can be no further doubt that, if Adenauer had wanted negotiations with the Soviets, they would have been possible without endangering Western integration.

Adenauer was not Bismarck; he never understood Russia. In March 1966, at the CDU national congress, when he, by his own admission and to the amazement of his friends in the party (the protocol indicates "applause and commotion"), "boldly" exclaimed that the Soviet Union had joined the ranks of nations "desiring peace," it was too late.[6] If he had recognized this in 1952, German history might have taken a different course.

Would a neutralized Germany necessarily have led to unstable conditions in central Europe, even to the sovietization of Germany in its entirety? Probably not. This was the publicly presented argument, but internal analyses—for example, by the Americans—suggest another view. And in 1953, Churchill decisively denied this reasoning. Adenauer's phrase, "Neutralization means sovietization," is in any case too brief, as is "Freedom or slavery." Many forms of neutrality exist, and Moscow did not demand withdrawal from the European Coal and Steel Community, as Adenauer concluded too quickly and without proof. The Soviets demanded renouncing *military* integration into the Western alliance, nothing more. All these issues would have needed to be negotiated with the Soviets. But only Adenauer's initiative could have overcome the rigidity in both East and West. His unyielding obstinacy and the inflexibility of his way of thinking prevented this from occurring: his worldview had remained unshakable since the end of the war. Added to this was his fear, and who can blame him, of losing the majority to the SPD in all-German elections (as the British and the French also feared), even though publicly he always maintained that this was not a concern.

Moreover, he underestimated the national strength of a reunified Germany, and this contributed to his outlook. To anchor the Federal Republic securely in the West and at the same time to protect it from the feared communist expansion by the Soviets—even at the cost of continuing division—this was Adenauer's declared goal. He continually warned against a neutralized, nonaligned Germany. On February 22, 1951, he stated: "What would the neutralization of Germany signify? The occupying troops would withdraw. For a certain time the semblance of a democratic nation would be preserved. The Soviets would exhaust all opportunities of undermining Germany from within with the help of the fifth column, in order to attain their goal by unscrupulous means."[7]

He unequivocally rejected even a neutral armed Germany between the two blocs. On May 23, 1952, three days before signing the treaties with the West, he expressed this view: "The worst thing for us is the thought that haunts many: that Germany should attempt to play its own game between the two great powers. This is an impossibility."[8]

Whether this was truly an impossibility remains the decisive question. It was primarily because of Adenauer's decision—and this can be stated with conviction—that negotiations with the Soviet Union did not take place; he immediately killed all initiatives to "probe" the note. He even sided with those opposed to proposing four-power talks for tactical reasons. Adenauer bears primary responsibility for making the all-German thorn a part of German politics since that time. His decision—which has come to light only since the documents were made available—to reject even the suggestion that Secretary of State Acheson made at the end of April weighs especially heavily.

From Adenauer's viewpoint, however, no opportunity was bungled in 1952 because the Soviet offer was not an opportunity at all. For him, integration into the West had absolute priority. His rejection, however, meant renouncing an active policy of reunification. In that "year of illumination [Klärung]," as Franz Josef Strauss accurately labeled 1952 looking back from the viewpoint of 1984,[9] those men from Adenauer's own ranks who gave priority to national unity and who wanted the Soviet offer to be at least examined—Kaiser, Ernst Lemmer, Gradl, Erik Blumenfeld, and apparently even von Brentano, to name only a few— could not, even in unison, prevail against Adenauer, so Schumacher, Heinemann, or journalists like Sethe did not even have a chance. Nothing reveals the problematic nature of this topic more clearly than Ulrich Noack's simple disqualification of this last group of men as "pillar saints."[10]

But this issue should not, and cannot, be made this simple. Waldemar Besson called Adenauer's refusal to examine the seriousness of the Soviet offer "the loss of his all-German innocence." The judgment of veteran diplomat Paul Frank comes down equally hard: this refusal contradicts a diplomat's professional ethos, "it constitutes a historic guilt concerning the idea of German unity, that in fact should have sealed forever the lips of those responsible when the discussion concerned reunification."[11] Nothing more can be added, especially not after examining the documents!

In the final analysis, the price of following the Western course "was morally so much more problematic because eighteen million East Germans had to pay it."[12] For everyone in the West clearly understood that the longer the division persisted, the further East and West would grow apart and the greater the "factors working against unity" would be. Undersecretary Allen in the British Foreign Office worried about these barriers at the end of July 1952. He mentioned economic, political, and psychological difficulties and also spoke about "the natural human tendency to become reconciled to existing situations."[13] The conclusion to be drawn from this was that the German problem would solve itself. Foreign Minister Eden may well have had similar thoughts, but the documents revealing his position were not released by the British government.

CHAPTER TEN

THE YEAR 1953: CHURCHILL, ADENAUER, AND REUNIFICATION

Whether Secretary of State Acheson seriously intended, as he claimed at the end of August 1952, to engage in confidential talks with the Soviets at a later date seems doubtful. Practically all prerequisites for an American–Soviet dialogue were missing. The Soviet Union was undergoing the last phase of Stalinism. Since the Korean War had begun in June 1950, the cold war had taken a dangerous turn. And the shooting in Korea continued in a conflict that the Americans—both Democrats and Republicans alike—viewed as the Kremlin's vicarious war.[1] The Korean war was an important theme in the American election campaign in the autumn of 1952, a campaign steeped in an atmosphere of fear and hysteria fueled by Senator Joseph McCarthy's anticommunist witch-hunt. Eisenhower conjured up a threat to America by a large tyrannical power that was brutal in its primitiveness and that had enslaved many millions of people and numerous nations from Poland and East Germany to China and Tibet. And Dulles condemned the

Democrats' policy of containing communism as negative, unproduc-
tive, and immoral and demanded instead an active "policy of liberation" that would give hope to the peoples enslaved by communism and
a goal to American foreign policy?[2] That this consistent anticommunist policy of liberation—the "New Look"—was little more than an
aggressive rhetoric of liberation, in practice differing little from Truman's policy, was not immediately recognized at that time either by
the United States' European allies or—as was to be expected—by the
Soviets.[3]

The new administration with Dwight D. Eisenhower as president,
the militantly anticommunist Richard Nixon as vice-president, and
John Foster Dulles as secretary of state presented itself to the world as
a government of cold warriors. To judge by their words, an intensification of the East–West conflict leading to unpredictable consequences
seemed unavoidable. In this situation, one man felt himself called to
lead the (Western) world more than ever before: the 78-year-old Winston S. Churchill. Since resuming leadership of British politics in November 1951, he had hoped to defuse the cold war, if not to end it
entirely, through negotiations at the highest level.

This was not the chimera of an aging statesman. Even if there can be
no doubt, as D. C. Watt has emphasized[4] and as the notes of Churchill's
personal physician confirm,[5] that Churchill wanted to be remembered
as a peacemaker as well as a wartime leader, there were other equally
important reasons for this policy. Great Britain was no longer the power
that had fought alongside the United States as a pro forma equal, and
Truman was not a partner with whom the intimacy of wartime could
be restored, as Churchill was painfully forced to recognize during his
visit with Washington leaders in January 1952. He did not even succeed
in getting them to abandon their plan of placing an American admiral
in charge of the Royal Navy in the Atlantic.[6]

Despite the changed circumstances, Churchill continued to view
Great Britain's interests against a global background. And as D. C. Watt
probably correctly presumed, Churchill apparently recognized at the
time that only a reduction in international tensions would enable Great
Britain to rebuild its strength to the point where it could face the
United States as an equal. The United States needed to be given a
reason to "keep America up to the mark"[7] and not to withdraw into
isolationism after becoming conscious of its own strength. However,
this could not occur at the cost of completely subjugating British interests to the bureaucracy in Washington.[8] What he was not successful in
obtaining from Truman, Churchill hoped to get from Eisenhower: a

stronger and livelier version of the good wartime relations. He envisioned picking up where he had left off when the British electorate had recalled him—as one of the "Big Three" at the Potsdam Conference. During these months, Churchill's thoughts revolved again and again around the events of the final months of his government in 1945 during which he was unable to persuade the Americans to accept his ideas. What was valid in 1945 was even more valid in 1953 in his opinion: America was very powerful, but also very clumsy. He wanted to bring the Americans discernment.[9]

On March 5, 1953, Stalin died. The legacy he left the Soviet Union and its European satellite states was an economy that was dangerously overburdened. Moreover, the Soviet Union was completely isolated in its foreign policy. For the West, the question was whether the new leadership under G. M. Malenkov and L. P. Beria with V. M. Molotov continuing as foreign minister would be prepared to pursue a policy of detente.

On March 11, Churchill seized the initiative on the Western side. He was primarily interested in learning what Eisenhower's attitude was toward the new Soviet leadership and toward the possibility of a meeting—jointly or independently. He had the feeling, as he wrote Eisenhower, that both of them might be called to account if no attempt was made to turn over a leaf so that a new page would be started with something more coherent on it than a series of casual and dangerous incidents at the many points of contact between the two divisions of the world. He did not doubt that Eisenhower was thinking deeply of this, which held the first place in his own thought.[10] On the following day, the rather sobering response came from Washington. Eisenhower rejected a meeting with the Kremlin leaders at the present time, since one should not give the Soviets the opportunity to stage a new "propaganda mill."[11]

Just a few days after Stalin's death, the new Soviet leadership initiated a curious activity: the "thaw." Western interpretations of this development diverged greatly. Was this merely a tactical move, or was it the beginning of a fundamental change in Soviet policy? On March 27, Molotov gave British ambassador Sir A. Gascoigne to understand that he wanted to involve himself in gaining the release of British diplomats being held prisoner in North Korea. At the same time, he proposed exchanging sick and wounded prisoners and resuming both cease-fire negotiations in Panmunjom and negotiations concerning aviation safety in Germany. Gascoigne's reaction was nevertheless reserved. He acknowledged that the new developments in Soviet policy could enhance the possibility of some slight easing of tension in the cold war, but he emphatically pointed out that this policy carried with it certain dangers, for "a really genuine change of heart which might bring about a basic change of policy is out of the question."[12]

This assessment of the situation was precisely in keeping with the Foreign Office's view. The leader of the Russian section prosaically summed up: "A few swallows do not make a summer."[13] In an analysis written for Foreign Minister Eden, Sir William Strang described the problems with the Soviet Union as "fundamental and a function of the two confronted worlds." The new Soviet policy might possibly be especially dangerous. In his opinion, the Soviets had decided to change their tactic only after recognizing that their rigid, intransigent, and aggressive policy led only to "the building up of the West morally and materially against them." Now they were hoping, where possible, to use a moderate policy: flexibility in small, unimportant—or possibly even a few more important—things to break up the anticommunist front and to bring the neutral states around to their side. In the past, the Soviets could always be trusted not to carry out any counterbalancing maneuvers that might be unpleasant for the West. Apparently this had changed. In any case, the new peace propaganda had more substance in it. From this, Strang concluded that the Western tactic should be to react as flexibly as possible, but without surrendering vital positions such as NATO. For he believed that "in this we may find the French to be very weak vessels." In conclusion it was decided to immediately recall Gascoigne to London for consultations.[14]

Churchill saw everything completely differently. For him, the news about the Soviet actions was "most favourable." Now he wanted to arrange a meeting between Eden and Molotov as quickly as possible. Recalling the ambassador for consultation was in his opinion a completely unnecessary step. He saw no advantage in "procedure for procedure's sake" and let Eden deliver the draft of a letter to Molotov in which Churchill described it as his greatest wish that Molotov and Eden, who had already conducted so many long and famous talks with one another in the past, would again come together for a "friendly and informal" meeting, possibly in Vienna. Such a talk "might lead us all farther away from madness and ruin." But even if nothing much should come of such a meeting, Churchill could not see that "any of us would be worse off." He again stressed that he wanted an interview not between Gascoigne and Molotov, but between Molotov and Eden. At a later stage, if all went well and everything broadened, "I and even Ike might come in too."[15]

The meeting between Eden and Molotov did not take place. At the beginning of April, Eden became seriously ill, needed surgery, and spent the next several months convalescing. Churchill decided, against the advice of his physician, to assume the leadership of the foreign office. In several personal messages to Molotov, he now attempted to explore the basis for initiating a dialogue with the new Soviet leaders. He interpreted the signals coming from Moscow as indicative of the Soviets' readiness for talks.[16]

At the beginning of May, he decided to establish direct contact with Moscow and, if necessary, to undertake a "solitary pilgrimage" there.[17] To this end, he planned to send a telegram to Molotov, but only after giving Eisenhower a chance to comment.[18] Eisenhower's commentary was immediate and completely negative.[19] On May 6, Churchill outlined his plans again and agreed not to travel to Moscow before the end of June.[20] Eisenhower responded on May 8 that he had tried to make clear that he of course recognized Churchill's right "to decide for himself in such matters." At the moment, however, he was far more concerned with the specific trouble spots of the world, namely, Korea, Southeast Asia, Laos, Iran, Egypt, Pakistan, and India. A thorough explanation of American policy toward these countries followed, together with critical comments on British policy. Eisenhower concluded: "As of this moment I still think that we have no recourse except to continue the steady buildup of Western morale and of Western economic and military strength. This is the great 'must' that confronts us all."[21]

Churchill persisted with his favorite idea: a summit conference. In his general foreign policy speech on May 11 in the House of Commons, he spoke in favor of quickly convening such a conference, as he had already done on April 20—now however, with greater urgency. This conference "should not be overhung by a ponderous or rigid agenda, or led into mazes and jungles of technical details, zealously contested by hoards of experts and officials drawn up in vast cumbrous array."[22]

At this point, those in the Foreign Office were themselves still uncertain what concrete goals Churchill wanted to pursue in the intended talks with the Soviets. That Germany would be a central theme was evident. And comments made by people ranging from the Soviet ambassador in Oslo to the Soviet secretary at the embassy in London suggest that the new Soviet leaders knew this as well.[23]

Churchill rarely intervened in the battle of the notes in 1952. Only a few indications of his opinion of this exchange exist. In March he demanded a memorandum and maps concerning the Oder–Neisse border. On the map, he expressly plotted that line in central Germany behind which the Anglo-American troops had withdrawn in July 1945 against his will. When the Soviet Union made concessions concerning the election issue in its second note from April 9, 1952, he limited himself to a brief commentary. That this did not resolve the entire matter for him can be seen from his remark that he was in no way clear about the basic question.[24] After the third Soviet note, he asked Strang to provide information about the Potsdam "decisions" that the Soviet government had referred to.[25] In the spring of 1953, this issue seemed clear to him: the Soviet Union would agree to a solution of the German question only if their security interests were adequately taken into account. In his speech on May 11, he thus became the first Western statesman to acknowledge publicly the security interests of the Soviet Union and to point to the treaty of Locarno as a possible path to agreement.[26] In fact, he did not exclude a neutralized reunified Germany as part of an overall settlement with the Soviet Union. The Foreign Office deemed it necessary to warn forcefully against following such a course:

> Acceptance of the Soviet aim of a "neutralized" Germany would mean a fundamental change in Allied policy pursued since 1947 and most recently restated in the Prime Minister's speech of May 11. Our present long-term policy, to which Dr. Adenauer has also dedicated himself, of attaching the Federal Republic and eventually a reunited Germany to the West cannot be reconciled with a return to the Potsdam policy, publicly rejected by us, of four-power control of a neutralised Germany. We have made good progress, but we need more time to produce solid results in Germany and Western Europe. As the Russians have pointed out, the abandonment of our present policies is the price of early agreement with the Soviet Union on the German problem. German reunification in freedom is therefore a long-term goal, as Dr. Adenauer informed the Prime Minister.

In the short run, it was feared that a return to Potsdam would lead either to Adenauer's defeat in the upcoming Bundestag elections and to a weak neutralist and probably socialist government or to the revival of extreme nationalism in the hope that a deal could be made with the Soviet Union. The Foreign Office dramatically described the long-term dangers of such a policy. All foreign troops must be withdrawn, all bases must be disbanded. Following the withdrawal of American troops, such a Germany would be so weak that it would be dependent on the mercy of the most powerful, ruthless, and determined power in Europe: the Soviet Union. In its entire history, Germany had never shown any particular vocation for neutrality, and a reunified Germany with a national army would use its economic and military power to bargain between East and West. The Russians had the former eastern territories to use as bait; the West had only the Saarland. Such a Germany, deprived of its anchor with the West, and with its center of gravity again in Berlin, would most probably become associated sooner or later with the Soviet bloc: "We should thus have created by our own action a grave danger to our own security." And then a quote from the Western note of May 13, 1952, was included. Neutralizing such a powerful country as Germany in the middle of Europe "would create a permanent state of tension and insecurity in the center of Europe."

But this was not enough; the effects on NATO, on connections between the United States and Europe, on Western European politics, on the relationship between Germany and France, and on Great Britain's economy were painted in the blackest colors. NATO's plans were based on (1) a forward strategy requiring the use of German territory and (2) a German defense contribution. If Germany were neutralized, both German troops and territory would be lost; allied troops would be withdrawn to France and the Netherlands, and American troops would probably be pulled out of Europe altogether, with incalculable consequences for the future of NATO itself and for American policy toward Europe. At best, NATO would no longer be an effective shield for Western Europe and Great Britain; at worst, Great Britain's security would entirely depend on the Soviets' goodwill. A neutralized Germany could no longer participate in the Western European policy of unification. Thus, this policy would collapse, German nationalism would revive, and Germany would again pose a danger for France and Western Europe. Yet another reason spoke out against a few policy:

A disarmed or neutralised Germany would be freed from heavy industrial, financial, manpower and other defense burdens, which would fall with even greater weight than at present upon the United Kingdom and its allies. German commercial competition, already a serious problem, would become a grave menace. . . . The struggle for Germany lies at the heart of the problem. The rearmament of the Federal Republic, her integration into Western Europe, the collective defence effort, the movement for European unity, are component parts of a whole. If we reverse our German policy, we may bring the whole structure tumbling about our ears and advance the frontiers of the Soviet bloc to the Rhine. Our object would presumably be to avert a third world war. But a war would be the almost certain result if Germany became a Soviet satellite or partner in an unholy alliance with the Soviet Union. We have a much better chance of averting a third world war with an effective Atlantic alliance and a united Europe in which for the time being three-quarters of Germany, rearmed but once again a healthy member of the Western family, plays its part.[27]

Churchill's response to this was rather reserved. He fully saw the awful consequences of a right-about-turn. It was certain to him that on the present course the world was moving steadily toward war. He had not yet come to any final conclusion in his own mind, but neither did he have any final inhibitions. In any case, however, his own sense of honor would keep him from abandoning Adenauer; that much he had promised the chancellor. A united Germany might become a second Czechoslovakia; this would not be good. The only hope would be the growing atomic superiority of the United States.[28]

Churchill's activity was viewed skeptically, not only in his own ranks but also in Washington and Paris. And Adenauer was plainly horrified. Adenauer's long-planned visit to London on May 14 and 15 did not change his views at all. Churchill assured him that Great Britain would stand by its obligations to the Federal Republic and would never reach an agreement behind the German's backs. Adenauer was more convinced than ever that Churchill did not properly understand the German problem and that he was not to be trusted in negotiations with the Soviets concerning Germany and Europe.[29] Not Churchill but Eisenhower was the partner who could be relied on. For this reason, on May 29 Adenauer sent Eisenhower a memorandum—not made public at the time—in which he again described his views on reunification.[30] As a further step, he presented the Bundestag with a five-point "Immediate Program for Reunification" that was approved by all the political parties, except the KPD, on June 10.[31]

On June 17, there was the workers' uprising in the GDR; for all those in the West who wanted to maintain the existing policy toward Germany and Russia, this was like manna from heaven. On June 19, when the three commanders of the Western sectors in Berlin, speaking on behalf of the three high commissioners, sharply protested the Soviet response,[32] Churchill was extremely annoyed. He asked Sir William Strang to explain how such a protest came to be made without his being informed in advance, and he wondered whether this implied that the Soviets "should have allowed the Eastern Zone to fall into anarchy and riot." He had the impression "that they acted with considerable restraint in the face of mounting disorder."[33] Selwyn Lloyd, minister of state in the Foreign Office, gave Churchill a remarkable answer on June 22. This secret memorandum indicates that the Foreign Office considered it time to give Churchill a lesson in the matter of German policy. What remained unexpressed in all actions at that time—and what critics of Western policy have always presumed—can be read here in black and white:

> Germany is the key to the peace of Europe. A divided Europe has meant a divided Germany. To unite Germany while Europe is divided, if practicable, is fraught with danger for many. Therefore, everyone—Dr. Adenauer, the Russians, the Americans, the French, and ourselves—feel in our hearts that a divided Germany is safer for the time being. But none of us dare say so openly because of the effect upon German public opinion. Therefore we all publicly support a united Germany, each on his own terms.[34]

Two weeks later, Churchill again took a position on the German question, in response to a cabinet presentation made by the Foreign Office.[35] In this memorandum to the acting foreign minister, he radically questioned what had previously become the basis of all Western policy toward Germany, almost like a natural law: the notion that a reunified, independent Germany would, in every case, become an ally of the Soviet Union or be controlled and sovietized by it: "Nothing will turn the German people from unity. ... We must face the fact that there will always be "a German problem" and "a Prussian danger." I am of opinion that a united, independent Germany would not become allies of Soviet Russia."

In Churchill's opinion, three reasons supported this assumption:

1. The character of the German people rises superior to the servile conditions of the Communist world.

2. They have had a potent object lesson in the fate of the Eastern zone and millions of witnesses will exist for many years to testify to the horrors of Communist rule, even exercised by Germans over Germans.

3. The hatred which Hitler focused against Bolshevism is strong in German hearts. The eyes of Germany are turned against Soviet Russia in fear, hate and intellectual antagonism. For France there is only contempt and pity. What is Alsace-Lorraine compared with Silesia and the Western Neisse in Russian hands? *I am sure that Germany will not, in the next 20 years, join with Russia against the*

West or lose her moral association with the Free Powers of Europe and America. That, at any rate, is the basis from which we ought to consider our terrible problem.[36]

Churchill could not convince his opponents. Adenauer, who probably suspected what was at stake, became a bitter opponent of Churchill in these weeks. Churchill's stroke in June made the game easier for Adenauer, for a summit conference of the three Western heads of state had to be canceled.

Instead, the three Western foreign ministers met in Washington in the middle of July. With an eye toward the upcoming elections, Adenauer pretended to be involved with all-German concerns,[37] and at his request, the Soviets were offered a foreign ministers' conference. This conference was doomed before it even began because nobody was prepared to deviate from the existing policy toward Germany even one iota. Adenauer had won the game: no summit conference was held, and the failure of the foreign ministers' conference in January and February 1954 was no surprise to anyone.

Churchill was deeply disappointed by this development. When he was shown the telegram from Washington in July, he drew the proper conclusion: "The French and the Americans intended the Four-Power Meeting to end in a breakdown."[38] In Churchill's opinion, the foreign ministers had "ruined everything." His hope had been the summit conference, a meeting with Malenkov.

The British prime minister was then convinced, as he himself put it, that they stood at a "turning point of the world."[39] That a man such as he, who even today has the reputation for being the first true "cold warrior," should have decided in 1953 to try to talk with the Soviets and thus was also ready to reconsider the German issue—in contrast to the bureaucrats in the Foreign Office—is one of the most exciting and, at the same time in view of the results, one of the most depressing findings to emerge from an examination of the documents.

Churchill's initiative came at an inauspicious time. Among those in the West who bore political responsibility, nobody other than himself was in a position to or was willing to depart from the already chosen policy toward Germany and Europe that had been agreed upon—with difficulties enough—and to seek out possible paths of detente. The thought is unimaginable that Adenauer might have become Churchill's partner rather than his embittered opponent.

For Adenauer, in contrast to Churchill, Stalin's death offered no new perspectives on reunification or on a conciliation of interests with the

Soviets. Indeed, the opposite was the case. On April 1, 1953, Adenauer warned the British high commissioner against falling under the illusion that there had been a Russian change of heart. The West should exploit the present situation energetically in order to get as much as possible from the Soviets. In Adenauer's view, the death of the Soviet dictator meant that "providence had given us a respite." The Soviets would be forced to tread warily for a while; the West should take advantage of this and resolutely push ahead with integration policy, since it now seemed fairly certain that "we should not be faced with any violent Russian action."[40]

Eisenhower was not capable of the highly personal form of diplomacy proposed by Churchill; he depended on his advisers and was possibly even more strongly anti-Soviet than Secretary of State Dulles.[41] The days of the "Big Three" of the Second World War, days that Churchill recalled with nostalgia, were definitely gone. And there was yet another factor that was not to be underestimated: in both East and West, foreign policy had grown more bureaucratized. The "underlinings," as Churchill disparagingly called them,[42] were not infrequently the ones determining policy. They would not declare war, but they were also singularly unsuitable peacemakers.

Nineteen fifty-three did not become a year of peace, nor did Churchill become the hoped-for peacemaker of the cold war. Practically everything in the West was against him, so he had to fail; his stroke in June did the rest. Churchill remained a lonely voice calling in the wilderness. Nevertheless, the question remains whether an opportunity was bungled a year after the Stalin Note, whether reunification in freedom on the basis of internationally supervised neutrality would have been attainable, possibly under conditions that would have exceeded those in the Stalin Note, if Soviet security needs could also have been satisfied. As long as the Soviet archives remain closed to Western researchers, answering this question will prove difficult.

Together with those "signals" confirming Churchill's view that it might very probably be worth talking to the new Soviet leaders, developments in the GDR—at least until June 17—also indicate the Soviets' willingness to negotiate again on the German question. We know that Vladimir Semenov, who was appointed high commissioner in the GDR at the beginning of June and who returned from Moscow to East Berlin on June 5, persuaded the SED leaders to abandon their policy of "constructing socialism" initiated in July 1952 and to prepare themselves for a loss of power through the upcoming reunification under democratic conditions.[43] On June 11, *Neues Deutschland* (New Germany) published the well-known resolution of June 9, in which the SED politburo acknowledged having made serious errors in economic policy and announced a "new course." "Through its resolution," the politburo envisioned, "the grand goal of establishing German unity, which demanded from both sides measures that would concretely facilitate the rapprochement between both parts of Germany." Significantly, the discussion was not of the "two German states" but "the two parts of Germany." And on June 13, the *Tägliche Rundschau* (Daily Survey), the official Soviet organ in the GDR, described the SED's resolutions as "aiming at the great goal of reunifying the German people in a unified, national German state." On the same day, by order of the SED politburo, all banners proclaiming the "construction of socialism" disappeared from the Berlin street scene.

June 17 brought an end to this development: "The attempt was abandoned because the chances of finding a negotiated solution to the German question that would be acceptable to the Soviets proved minimal and because the first steps had already touched off a crisis that potentially endangered the entire Soviet East European empire."[44] From this point on, the GDR was apparently no longer dispensable (although, in view of the missing sources, the question remains how the Soviet Union's offer of reunification made at the end of 1954 and the beginning of 1955 and designed to prevent the Federal Republic's accession into NATO are to be evaluated).[45]

On June 26, Beria, the head of the Soviet secret police, fell from power; on December 23, 1953, he was executed. At the fifteenth session of the SED central committee from July 24 to 26, 1953, Walter Ulbricht complained that Beria had wanted to "sell out" the GDR in negotiations with the West.[46] In 1957, Khrushchev extended this reproach to former Soviet President Malenkov, following Malenkov's overthrow in 1955 and his exclusion from the Soviet Politburo in 1957 for being a member of an "antiparty group," a group to which, Molotov also belonged. In 1961, when this group was condemned anew at the Twenty-Second Communist Party Congress, Khrushchev repeated his reproach.[47] On the other hand, Semenov, who was also reportedly "prepared to sell out" the GDR, was never reprimanded and has continued his diplomatic career up to the present day with full honors. For Richard Löwenthal, this fact provides "conclusive proof" that Semenov's instructions came not from Beria alone nor from Beria and Malenkov, but from the Politburo itself. What failed on June 17, in Löwenthal's opinion, was an official experiment of Soviet policy and not the private intrigue of individual Soviet leaders. However, to those who would conclude from this that June 17 was itself the decisive cause of this failure, he suggests that

> such a conclusion would focus on the immediate cause of the Soviet change of mind and would overlook the actual causative factors— the intransigence of Western, even of West German, foreign policy in the critical months following Stalin's death. Especially for the Federal Republic, it is a question not of a failure due to incompetence but of a policy completely consciously pursued by its first chancellor.... The division of Germany became fixed—and thus became the keystone in the division of Europe.[48]

CHAPTER ELEVEN

A RETROSPECTIVE LOOK
AT ADENAUER'S POLICY
Integration of West Germany with
the West—No Reunification

When we look back to 1952 and 1954, what can Adenauer be accused of? In the opinion of Hans-Peter Schwarz, "at most . . . that he opted for security in the circumstances of 1952 and 1953 and did not temporize [*temporieren*] with the Western treaties." Whatever Schwarz might mean by *temporieren*, he immediately added, "At that time, a German chancellor could not have risked doing any more than he did, and even what he did do would not have been easy."[1] Only the path to Western integration was easy to follow, and although the particulars presented many difficulties, Adenauer astutely solved these. Commitment to the West was what the Western powers wanted. Any other option would have been more difficult for a German politician, but in the interest of unity, another option would certainly have been more worthwhile. Venturing to pursue this option, therefore, deserved a try; the German chancellor could have risked more—if he had wanted to.

This attempt was not made, for, as Hans-Peter Schwarz explained,

"Following a sober evaluation of the situation, political reason recommended keeping the bird in the hand rather than chasing after the two birds of reunification in the bush."[2] This statement is questionable. Did political reason really advocate this, and were the two birds really sitting in the bush? In 1952, when Secretary of State Acheson wanted to begin talks with the Soviets, Adenauer could have made the attempt without endangering anything, even though Acheson had his own reasons for making the offer.

In the critical uncertainty of the Korean summer of 1950, Adenauer recognized the unique historical moment and used the newly won authority of the Federal Republic to influence the great powers with his proposal to allow the Germans to provide a military contingent. This resulted in the Western powers' decision in principle that the West Germans should be rearmed. Up to the spring of 1952, German authority made further decisive gains, although the Occupation Statute continued in force. Without this increase in German influence, which was the policy pursued up to that time, the Soviet offer would never have been made. In this respect, Adenauer's policy up to this point must unquestionably be applauded, even though its goal was not reunification. Nevertheless, it was only with a German military contribution that the Federal Republic attained such an important position in the Western system of defense that the Western powers were not prepared to relinquish it voluntarily.

But when Stalin's offer arrived, Adenauer could have played this German card—indeed, should have played it in the national interest. Even if the result had consisted only in proving that the Soviet offer was merely a stratagem, much would have been gained. To again quote Carlo Schmid, "Some friends of the fatherland who are today concerned about Germany's future would [have been] spared the nostalgic glance backward to 1952."[3] Thus, not the least of these gains would have been preventing this note from haunting us more than thirty years later, an effect Adenauer apparently did not foresee at the time. We know the result of his policy: the history of the Federal Republic became a singular success, but the price for this was the continuing division of the country. With his policy, Adenauer at the time slammed the door to unity. The same success, the same measure of freedom, but for *all* Germans is a *united* Germany? Was this not in any case worth a try? The reasons Adenauer made the decision he did and not a different one have been thoroughly discussed.

If Adenauer ever truly believed that one day, from a position of strength, he could dictate to the Soviet Union the conditions for reunification and possibly a reorganization of Eastern Europe, and that he could force it to capitulate, to give up its war booty without a quid pro quo—perhaps even by appealing to law, as though the Germans had not lost the war[4]—then for him, this was just as great an illusion as his confidence in Western support for his policy based on faith in Article 7 of the Bonn Convention. The Western powers had no serious interest in reunification, not to mention any possible corrections in the Oder–Neisse line or the return of lost eastern territories. For the Western powers, the Oder–Neisse line had been settled de facto since Potsdam; publicly, however, this theme continued to be used to keep false hopes alive among the Germans and, especially, to prevent negotiations with the Soviet Union.

The Western powers' public professions favoring reunification were only lip service, nothing more than compulsory diplomatic exercises. Internally, their views had a different appearance, as was expressed, for example, by the majority of high-ranking officials who met at the U.S. State Department on April 1, 1952. The Western powers' primary concern was to strengthen the West Germans' military and economic ties to the West so that, as President Eisenhower stated in December 1953, "they could not break loose."[5] Dividing Germany and allying the Federal Republic to the West were considered the best solution to the German question, but in view of public opinion in (West) Germany, nobody could say this openly. In public pronouncements, even in the Bonn Convention, the West obliged itself to pursue a policy of reunification, while at the same time very consciously—and entirely in keeping with Adenauer's views—adding conditions that were obviously not going to be acceptable to the Soviet Union.

Surprisingly, Adenauer clung to the European Defense Community to the end, although by 1952 indications were already increasing that France would not ratify this treaty. The vote of the French National Assembly on August 30, 1954, hit him hard; at the time, he considered resigning, not without reason.

If necessary, the topic of a West European federal state could have been debated, but the "alternative solution"—including the Federal Republic in NATO—was definitely not worth killing all chances for reunification. That Adenauer was successful in getting the majority to accept his policy of Western integration as the only possible course for (West) German policy and simultaneously the only and shortest path to reunification—something even the Americans doubted in 1952— was a remarkable accomplishment. At the same time, it was the lie of a lifetime for the Federal Republic, but one with which the population easily came to terms, completely in keeping with Bonn politics. The apparent threat of communism, the iron curtain, and the defense of freedom as well as of a new prosperity—one easily allowed oneself to be reassured. One quickly accepted this interim arrangement and, as an expression of the "moral distress" caused by the all-German issue, put candles in the window once a year in remembrance of "the brothers and sisters in the [Eastern] zone." These times are gone; the topic of a lie of a lifetime will probably be discussed anew by a new generation. We can look forward to the answers.

In Paris, two days after the Federal Republic joined NATO, Adenauer expressed the conviction: "We are now members of the strongest alliance in history. It will bring us reunification."[6] If he really believed this, he was again mistaken. Integration into the West and reunification were mutually exclusive. In internal discussions among the Western allies, this fact was repeatedly stated in just this way with great openness.[7] Adenauer's critics frequently pointed this out, and it is difficult to imagine that Adenauer was not aware of the consequences of his policy.

Those who were perceptive saw that what might have been possible before joining NATO became more and more of an illusion later. What Adenauer presented as an important step toward reunification became the final goal for the Western powers. The victors prepared for coexistence on the basis of a divided Germany. From that point on, time definitely worked not *for* reunification, as Adenauer possibly expected, but *against* it.

In 1965, four years after the construction of the Berlin Wall, Konrad Adenauer published the first volume of his *Erinnerungen*. The dedication he gave to this first and to all additional volumes was a curious one: "To my fatherland." But what exactly was Adenauer's fatherland? many people wondered at the time. Was it the Germany of 1937, or the two German states of 1949, or only the Federal Republic? The answer to this question also speaks to the closely related issues of how serious Adenauer truly was about the reunification of which he so frequently spoke. What remains from his assertion that the shortest and only true path to reunification was to integrate the Federal Republic into the Western alliance?

During the Federal Republic's fortieth anniversary celebration, the debate concerning Adenauer's role as "patriot" dampened the festive spirit of the occasion. The result was distressing for Adenauer and his supporters. Simply stated, Adenauer did not want reunification. In retrospect, all his protestations to the contrary have been shown to be merely a strategic ruse, the lie of a lifetime for the Federal Republic. Adenauer was not a "reunification chancellor," nor was he a chancellor for all the Germans. For him, integration into the West had absolute priority. An especially interesting document in the Public Record Office in London substantiates this view. This document is a top secret note written by Sir Ivone Kirkpatrick, who had been appointed permanent undersecretary of state in December 1953. Kirkpatrick composed this note on December 16, 1955, after a meeting with the German ambassador to London, Hans von Herwarth. He considered this document of such importance that he kept it in his safe and did not allow any copies to be made. He showed it only to Foreign Minister Harold Macmillan, whose commentary is noteworthy: "I think he [Adenauer] is right."

In 1955, there seemed to be some movement in international politics. On May 15, Austria was granted the State Treaty; the occupying troops were to withdraw, and Austria was to be free. Were the Soviets using this as a signal to Bonn, or was this the end of a series of developments? In either case, Adenauer was invited to Moscow in June; in July, a summit conference of the heads of state and government took place in Geneva in a completely relaxed atmosphere. The Soviets revealed another side to their nature; the "spirit of Geneva" drifted over the political stage and had its effect on the German question.

On July 19, 1955, Eden had a "frank and intimate talk" with N. A. Bulganin outside the conference room, which was "in a long experience of talks with Russians . . . the most important and certainly the frankest conversations that I have known," as he later told the cabinet. Bulganin plunged into the problem of Germany. He explained in familiar terms how real the Soviet fears of a German recovery were. Almost every family in Soviet Russia, including his own, had suffered some personal loss. Eden replied that they in Britain also had no reason to feel tenderly toward the Germans after the experience of two wars. But one had to look to the future, and whatever the fear of Germany had been, he could not believe that in the nuclear age Germany could really be a formidable danger to Russia. Bulganin, however, would not altogether accept this. He admitted that the Germans might not be able to make hydrogen bombs, but after all they could be given to them. Then Bulganin said that he wanted to say something to Eden "which he had said to nobody else":

It was really not possible for his Government to return to Moscow from this Conference having agreed to the immediate unification of

Germany. They were a united Government and reasonably solidly based in the country but this was something that Russia would not accept and if they were to agree to it, neither the Army nor the people would understand it and this was no time to weaken the Government.... In further discussion with him, and later with Khrushchev it emerged that while they could not agree to the unification of Germany now, they might be prepared to consider terms of reference for the Foreign Secretaries, which would contemplate such unification together with other compensating conditions.[8]

Adenauer's mistrust was aroused at Geneva. If the Soviets had hoped to do business with Adenauer, they thoroughly deceived themselves. In Adenauer's view, Khrushchev and Bulganin were only "uneducated and primitive peasants," as he confided to the Western ambassadors during his visit to Moscow in September. The result was predictable: the establishment of diplomatic relations with Moscow, and thereby the recognition of Germany's dual statehood, was to be made in exchange for the oral pledge to release German prisoners of war. Nothing more came out of this visit. Not surprisingly, in November, at the foreign ministers' conference in Geneva, it finally became clear that no further movement could be expected on the German question from the Soviet side. What Adenauer's critics had warned against was now obvious to everyone: Western integration excluded reunification. Even Adenauer's closest advisers, who had apparently believed that this was not the case, began to have doubts. Thus Herbert Blankenhorn in the British Foreign Office wondered whether one did not indeed need to return to the Soviet concept of a neutralized, unified Germany if unity was ever to be achieved at all. In the Foreign Office, this touched off an alarm. If Blankenhorn was already in such a "dangerously appeasing mood," what would the reactions in Bonn be?

The concerns in the Foreign Office were unfounded. The following document explains why this was so and offers a response to the question posed earlier about the nature of Adenauer's "fatherland." With unusual openness, this note from Kirkpatrick makes it clear that reunification was not a serious concern for Adenauer. His fear that this position might become known in Germany provides an interesting backdrop. The lie was sustained and became the lie of a lifetime:

> The German ambassador told me yesterday that he wished to make a particularly confidential communication to me on this subject. I would recollect that I had told him on my return from Geneva that I had come to the conclusion that we might eventually have to

be more elastic than the Americans were prepared to be and that we might have to move to a position in which we declared that, provided Germany was unified by means of free elections and provided the unified German Government had freedom in domestic and foreign affairs, we should sign any reasonable security treaty with the Russians.

The Ambassador told me that he had discussed this possibility very confidentially with the Chancellor. Dr. Adenauer wished me to know that he would deprecate reaching this position. The bald reason was that Dr. Adenauer had no confidence in the German people. He was terrified that when he disappeared from the scene a future German Government might do a deal with Russia at the German expense. Consequently he felt that the integration of Western Germany with the West was more important than the unification of Germany. He wished us to know that he would bend all his energies towards achieving this in the time which was left to him, and he hoped that we would do all in our power to sustain him in this task.

In making this communication to me the Ambassador naturally emphasised that the Chancellor wished me to know his mind, but that it would of course be quite disastrous to his political position if the views which he had expressed to me with such frankness ever became known in Germany.[9]

There was no unification. In effect, and without ever admitting it to each other, much less to the public, the Western allies and the Russians agreed to a stalemate in Germany. That agreement alone was a big step toward reducing tensions, at least for the time being.

Even before the Berlin Wall was built, John F. Kennedy had privately been skeptical on the question of German reunification. As Frank Cash, who was in the German Office of the State Department at the time, recalls, the Kennedy White House decided very early that the phrase "German reunification" could "no longer be included in drafts for use by the President." As a result, the State Department was compelled to adopt such "circumlocutions as 'self-determination for the German people' or 'freedom of choice for the German people.' "

With the construction of the Berlin Wall on August 13, 1961, the division of the country was cemented in the literal sense of the word and was accepted as a stable element in an unstable world—by the Western powers and the Soviet Union alike. Those who had placed their hopes in the Western powers now became painfully aware of this. On August 18, 1961, the chairman of the CDU/CSU in the Bundestag,

Heinrich Krone, wrote in his diary: "The hour of great disillusionment. The German people expected more than a protest note from the West. Those who question our reliance on the West are speaking out."[10] At the end of 1961, he bitterly took stock:

> The wall divides Germany and provides the border between the communist East and the free world. And, what we never wanted to believe [has happened], American policy has recognized this border. What the Western powers promised us in treaties, that they would not rest until Germany was again one nation and one country—all that is meaningless at the moment, whatever may happen in the future.

His judgment of the West Germans was also harsh: "We must stop sleeping. We are growing fat in our prosperity and over there the Germans are starving in their hearts and souls."[11]

What had occurred was now obvious to all and confirmed the prediction the CDU politician Ernest Lemmer made in May 1952 at a party discussion of whether to support the Western treaties and to oppose the Stalin Note: "The year 1952 will go down in history as the year of the historic division of Germany."[12]

It is a truism that Germany lies "in the middle of Europe"; up to 1945, the middle of Europe was marked by the bankruptcy of German policy. At the end of German hubris stood disaster, the nemesis of power. From this came Adenauer's basic decision to turn (West) Germany's face once and for all toward the West: his goal was complete linkage with the West. His success in bringing about this linkage is demonstrated by the five-volume *Geschichte der Bundesrepublik Deutschland* (History of the Federal Republic of Germany) that has recently been completed; soon it will probably also be possible to visit a "House of the History of the Federal Republic of Germany" in Bonn, a project initiated by the current chancellor, Helmut Kohl, who sees himself as Adenauer's "political descendant." This linkage is also reflected in the reception that the diplomatic representatives of the Federal Republic abroad hold each year, on the instructions of the German Foreign Office, on May 23. This reflects a country's search for identity, in which May 23 has become, inappropriately, a substitute for a national holiday.

But Germany is more than just the Federal Republic of Germany; Germany belonged and belongs to West, *and* East. After 1945, the Germans no longer threatened the peace; Germany's central position did not need to be a curse but could have been an opportunity for developing a peaceful policy in the East–West conflict. Viewed from this perspective, why was Adenauer's fundamental decision not questioned even in the 1950s? Was it not primarily a decision favoring the interests of the Western victors? In 1952 and 1953, another path might have been possible, but not even an attempt was made.

The price for Adenauer's decision must ultimately be paid by eighteen million East Germans. Even though Adenauer clearly did not want this to occur, this remains a fact that is all too often overlooked by those who unconditionally affirm his policy. His decision was such a momentous one especially, but not solely, for this reason.

The battles of the fifties have been fought; reunification is no longer a topical issue and is not considered an urgent problem on the world political agenda. Nevertheless, the Stalin Note does not belong to a finished epoch of German postwar history; it remains a national problem with which one has not yet come to terms. Nothing reveals this better than a representative opinion poll conducted in 1984 by the Allensbach Institute. According to this survey, 53 percent of the population in the Federal Republic above the age of sixteen favored reunification in a nonaligned Germany, a Germany such as Stalin proposed in 1952.[13]

But one should not make too much of the results of such a poll: the hard facts of East–West relations always carry more weight than all the Germans' nostalgia for Germany. Today the issue can be only an orderly parallel and—hopefully—cooperative course for the two German states. The lost opportunities of history do not recur.

Still, some concluding speculation is allowed: even though the GDR and the Federal Republic in 1985 no longer have their provisional status of 1952 and the international conditions have also thoroughly changed, it remains to be seen whether history in this case will not indeed repeat itself, whether a West German government will not one day find itself in a situation similar to that in which Adenauer found himself in 1952. Then we shall see what decision will be made. Soviet policy has staying power; if anyone can still play the "German card," then it is probably only the Soviet Union.

APPENDIX

DOCUMENT ONE

TELEGRAM FROM JOHN McCLOY
TO DEAN ACHESON
March 12, 1952

West German reaction to Soviet demarche appears thus far to be grat-ifyingly level-headed. We get this from conversations with officials and from scanning this morning's press. Separate telegram on press reactions is being sent.

Fortunately for us, most Germans have few illusions about Russia and Bolshevism. Most Germans who learned of Soviet proposals therefore approached them with skepticism. Editors have quickly pointed out defects in Soviet note from German point of view, particularly territorial limitations. Soviet terms were in general so overdrawn as to be implausible.

Notwithstanding this, we must recognize that issue to which Kremlin directed this propaganda blast—German unity—is one regarding which German people are sensitively responsive. That no (repeat no)

SOURCE: DoS 662.001/3-1252. Incoming Telegram No. 1939 from Bonn, Priority, Secret.

dramatic response has thus far been elicited is due not to error in Soviet appeal to unity issue but to ingrained German suspicion of moves originating from East.

Dangers inherent in Soviet move appear to us as follows:

1. Many Germans feeling strongly on unity issue will, despite conscious skepticism, wishfully hope that Kremlin proposal might at least be given a try. Natural tendency of Germans to look back over their shoulders at unity as a first priority may be fortified and there develop an increased inclination to drag their feet as we seek them to advance toward integration with West. Because these sentiments are at once so deep-rooted and so amorphous, we cannot be sure that initial sane reaction which we now observe to Kremlin demarche will remain steady.

2. Soviet terms for peace treaty obviously increase Federal Republic's bargaining power in contractual negotiations while paradoxically emphasizing provisional character of Federal Republic thereby weakening government's position.

3. If our reaction to Soviet note appears to be negative and to foreclose possibility of German unity, Kremlin proposals will come to exercise an appeal which they do not now possess and task of persuading West Germans to go along with integration will be critically impeded.

We offer following suggestions for consideration by Department in its preparation of reply to Soviet Government.

1. We should indicate that we are gratified to note that Soviet Government has come to agree with us regarding importance of taking as a first step toward peace settlement creation of an All-German Government through democratic processes. This obviously means All-German elections.

2. We have participated in creating of a UN commission to examine simultaneously in Federal Republic and Soviet Zone possibility of holding such elections and to report findings to the UN.

3. We have forwarded to Soviet Government a Federal Republic draft law for holding of such elections.

4. We await indication from Soviet Government that it will support these moves and hope that answer will be in affirmative.

5. Being serious in our desire to establish German unity as the indis-

pensable first step toward peace, being interested in practical progress toward this goal and seeing no useful end being served by encouraging Soviet exercises in sophistry such as have been witnessed at the Palais Rose and through Austrian peace treaty negotiations, we do not propose to engage now in a discussion of the inadequacies of Soviet proposals for a German peace treaty.

To give reply positive tone first two points should be heavily emphasized and fifth played down.

Finally, we would recommend against officially going into any details regarding peace treaty terms proposed by Soviet Government. However, we do not feel that this should preclude active background guidance to press and radio.

We consider reply to Soviet note should be issued as soon as possible to avoid appearance to Germans of lack of allied resolutions.

DOCUMENT TWO

POLICY PLANNING STAFF MEMORANDUM FROM M. SCAMMON AND R. W. TUFTS TO PAUL NITZE

March 14, 1952

Outline of Factors Bearing on the Western Reply to the Soviet Note on Germany

I. *The Soviet Purpose*
A. We do not know, of course, the real motivation of the Soviet note. There is general agreement, however, that it should be taken seriously, both because it has the ring of considered policy rather than propaganda and because it omits, superficially at least, demands for four power control of Germany and the Ruhr on which the Russians have been insistent heretofore and apparently reverses the previous Soviet positions on German armed forces and military production. The Russians probably believe that their move can be exploited in more than one

SOURCE: National Archives, Washington, Record Group 59, 762 A. 00/3-1452.

way—in other words, the purpose for which the move will in
fact be exploited is partly dependent on our reaction. We should
keep the possibility in mind that the Russians:

1. might be willing to negotiate a German settlement on this
   basis;
2. might be trying to influence the Germans to go slow on the
   integration of Western Germany into the Western system;
3. might be trying to involve the Western powers in endless
   negotiations a la Panmunjom—as a means of blocking
   Western Germany's integration into the Western system
   and thus Western European integration in general;
4. might be trying to lay a basic political position which they
   feel they can live with over a long period and which they
   can profitably exploit over the long term;
5. might be laying the political basis for an early major shift in
   Soviet policy, not necessarily related to Germany alone.
   What such a shift might be is anybody's guess; it might
   range from a policy of preparation for a long contest in the
   West, beginning with a relaxation of tensions on European
   questions, through consolidation of the Soviet system by a
   new effort to evict the Western powers from Berlin, all the
   way to aggressive action probably involving war.

II. *The Purpose of the Western Response*
   A. Broadly speaking, we want to respond in such a way as:
      1. to avoid the traps and pitfalls, if any (and there almost
         certainly are);
      2. to run a litmus test on Soviet intentions; and
      3. to push, if possible, towards our objectives with respect to
         Germany, Western Europe, and the Soviet system.
   B. Broadly speaking, there are four possible types of Western re-
      sponse:
      1. Outright rejection.
      2. A propaganda-type rejection (i.e., renewed expressions of the
         Western desire for German unity and a German peace treaty
         accompanied by conditions which are designed to appear as
         plausible as possible and to be unacceptable to the Rus-
         sians).
      3. Request for clarification.
      4. Counter-proposals designed to call the Soviet hand (i.e., to
         make the Soviets decide whether to proceed promptly with

the creation of an all-German Government and possibly with the withdrawal of forces or to indicate that they will not so proceed).

C. *Traps and Pitfalls.* Outright or propaganda rejection might lead us straight into a Soviet trap. It must be presumed that the Soviet rulers have considered the possibility that we will reject their proposals and have a plan for exploiting such a Western counter-move. Whatever their desired aim is, they could exploit a Western rejection by trying to influence the Germans along the lines indicated in I.A.2 above or laying a political foundation along the lines indicated in I.A.4 and 5. The most obvious and probably the immediate aim of the Russians is to elicit a request for clarification, to which they could respond in such a way as to make it very difficult for us to avoid negotiations, with their further aims dependent in large part on the course of the negotiations. This is the most obvious purpose because their note is not an easy one to reject as mere propaganda or old stuff. It is probably their immediate purpose because it offers not only short-term advantages in delaying action by the West but also preserves the opportunity for realizing long-term advantages if the Western position in negotiations provides any openings of this kind.

D. *A Test of Soviet Intentions.* A request for clarification will probably not give us a clear and early test of Soviet intentions, no matter how carefully it is worded. We might eventually learn what we want to know but only after long negotiations, which we want to avoid. A quick test of Soviet intentions can probably be obtained only by a counter-proposal specifically designed to call the Soviet hand. It goes without saying that it will be extremely difficult to draft a satisfactory counter-proposal. This problem is taken up in Section IV of this memorandum. What is clear is that if a counter-proposal is made, it must be one with which we can live and which will, if possible, advance us, whether accepted or rejected by the Soviet Union, toward our objectives.

III. *Western Objectives*

A. If a Western counter-proposal is rejected by the Soviet Union, the Soviet reaction should greatly assist us in making progress on our present policies in Western Europe. It would again demonstrate that German unity is not a real alternative to our present policies and underline once more the phoneyness of Soviet proposals. Soviet rejection is the probable outcome of our move—if that move is well planned. The recent national intelligence estimate, which OIR [Office of Intelligence Research, State Department] endorses, reaches the conclusion that the Soviet Union is not willing at this time to sacrifice its position in Eastern Germany for the sake of possible long-run advantages with respect to Germany as a whole.

B. Nevertheless, if a counter-proposal is made, there is an off chance that it will be accepted by the Russians. The question which immediately arises is whether a settlement on the basis of a unified, independent, and neutral Germany is consistent with our objectives.

C. This leads to the following questions:

1. Are we likely to have success in carrying out our present policies if in addition to our present difficulties we add whatever difficulties would be caused by rejection of the Soviet proposals? It is only by rejection that we can be sure that we will not be trapped into frustrating negotiations or into a settlement on the basis of a unified Germany, with all that that implies. In answering this question, we must bear in mind that we have been having great difficulties and that great difficulties loom ahead in France and Germany and elsewhere on the continent. Rejection of the Soviet proposals would intensify these difficulties. The probable result would be, at best, even more halting rate of progress toward our present goals than we have been making and, at worst, a stymie. However, halting progress and perhaps even a stymie would be preferable to a basically unsound European situation. Would a settlement on the basis of a unified, independent, and neutral Germany create such a situation or would it be consistent with U.S. interests, and, if so, under what circumstances? We have to consider this question even though we estimate that the chances of a German settlement on this basis are probably not more than one in ten.

D. *The consequences of a settlement involving a unified, independent, and neutral Germany.* The United States would be confronted with a choice between two major lines of development of its European policy. First, we might seek to maintain NATO and undertake to align Germany's interests with the

West or at least with the maintenance of its independence from the Soviet Union. Second, we might seek to develop a unified Western Europe which would, as a bloc, play a strong neutral role and revise NATO so that the U.S. and U.K. guaranteed the security of the bloc without receiving reciprocal guarantees.

1. *Maintenance of NATO.* It is possible that the French reaction to a unified, independent, and neutral Germany would be an even greater interest in the maintenance and development of NATO than it now has. It is most unlikely that Germany would, so long as it remained weak, make a deal with the Soviet Union. The more likely development, and one which should be able to assist indirectly, is that Germany would seek to develop enough strength to gain, in light of its recognition of our interests in preventing its domination by the Soviet Union, a sense of security. If this came about, there would then indeed be the possibility of deals with the Soviet Union, but these would be deals which Germany would conclude only if they improved its position vis-a-vis the Soviet Union. There might be a real advantage, in terms of our long run interests with respect to the Soviet Union and to world peace, in having an independent Germany which could so negotiate with the Soviet Union, for in this case the Soviet Union might not be as reluctant to make concessions to Germany as to a united and in its view necessarily hostile Western bloc which included Germany. On the whole it is probably in the long run interest of the U.S. if new power centers can be established and if the present East-West conflict can be replaced by an interplay of interests between several power centers. We need not fear Germany so long as we maintain a strong atomic capability.

2. *Western European Unification.* Alternatively, it might be possible to push forward with the creation of a new Western European power center, which would not be formally allied to the U.S. and the U.K., but which, for a variety of reasons, would be impelled to remain on friendly terms with us and to concentrate its available energies on improving the security of its position in the East. This would involve the alteration of NATO from a reciprocal undertaking to a pledge by the U.S. and the U.K. to regard an attack on Western Europe as an attack on themselves. Such a development would also be consistent with our long-term interests. Which of these

two lines we could and should follow would depend largely on the preferences of the continental countries, especially France and Germany.

E. It should be emphasized once again that the probable results of a Western counter-proposal will be, first, to reveal that the Soviet Union is, at the moment, bluffing and thus, second to assist us in moving ahead with our present policies. Furthermore, even if the Soviet Union should be willing to make a German settlement, it seems unlikely that it will be willing to make one in the near future. The Soviet Union may see its choice as one between a German settlement and a preventive war, but it probably does not regard this as a choice which has to be made urgently. It may feel that the choice depends largely on the terms it could get for a German settlement. From this it is concluded that we should respond to the Soviet note in a way which indicates that we prefer a German settlement to war, if the terms of settlement are reasonable, but our price should be high enough to reflect confidence in the basic strength of our general position and the basic weakness of the Soviet position in Germany.

F. If we go down this course, it will be of the greatest importance to move as rapidly as possible on the contractual arrangements and the EDC-EDF [European Defense Community-European Defense Force] arrangements, for it is only by demonstrating that we have a real alternative that we can effectively put pressure on the Soviet Union (whose alternatives are less favorable) to negotiate a German settlement.

IV. Form of a Reply to the Note of the USSR

The essence of our reply to the Soviet note of 10 March should be as follows:

1. This Government welcomes the suggestions of the Soviet Government with respect to preparing in the nearest future an agreed draft peace treaty with Germany.

2. This Government agrees with the Soviet Government's view that any such agreed peace treaty must be worked out with direct participation of Germany in the form of an all-German Government.

3. In order to further the desires of the Soviet Government to proceed with discussions of such a treaty in the nearest

future, this Government proposes that steps be undertaken immediately to organize the holding of democratic all-German elections on Sunday, November 16, 1952, or on such other similar date as may be agreed, to select an all-German Constituent Assembly.

4. In the organization of these elections this Government proposes that the laws, ordinances, administrative orders, and regulations concerning the election of the German Constituent Assembly of 1919 be applied, with the addition of a system of four-power control comparable to that employed in the Berlin city elections of October, 1946. To provide appropriate four-power responsibility in this matter, this Government proposes that the three High Commissioners of Great Britain, France, and this Government join with the head of the Soviet Control Commission not later than April 1, 1952, to establish such authority as may be deemed advisable for these purposes.

5. Lest there be any misunderstanding of the firm intention of the responsible powers to proceed resolutely to the election of a democratic German Constituent Assembly, this Government proposes that each power guarantee in its zone the terms of paragraphs three and four of the political provisions of the Soviet Government's draft treaty of 10 March, namely—

> (3) Democratic rights must be guaranteed to the German people to the end that all persons under German jurisdiction without regard to race, sex, language, or religion enjoy the rights of man and the basic freedoms including freedom of speech, press, religious persuasion, political conviction, and assembly.
>
> (4) Free activity of democratic parties and organizations must be guaranteed in Germany with the right of freedom to decide their own internal affairs, to conduct meetings and assembly, to enjoy freedom of press and publication.

6. This Government is prepared to presume that the implementation of paragraph five above will be in effect from April 1, 1952. Should any of the powers concerned fail to guarantee these terms in its zone of responsibility, this Government would feel that the other participating powers would

automatically be freed from any further commitments with respect to the holding of an election to an all-German Constituent Assembly. Should any of the powers concerned not maintain the guarantees envisaged in paragraphs five above *after* the holding of elections to the all-German Constituent Assembly, this Government would feel that such failure would be an effective cancellation of the elections and would automatically dissolve the Constituent Assembly.

DOCUMENT THREE

TELEGRAM FROM CECIL LYON
TO DEAN ACHESON
March 15, 1952

From European Affairs Division.

Preliminary analysis of Soviet motives and intentions underlying recent peace treaty note follows.

Apparently general agreement here that prime reason for approach is effort to retard West German militarization and integration with Western Europe. We entirely concur.

Varying opinions exist, however, as to whether and how far Soviets might go, toward making concessions to Western demands, in order finally reach agreement on unification of Germany. These vary from one extreme view that no concessions will be made and that entire approach is propaganda effort; to other, that concessions might be made even to point where West could accept agreement. On balance scepti-

SOURCE: DoS 662.001/3-1552. Incoming Telegram No. 1139 from Berlin, Confidential Security Information.

cism remains dominant, though perhaps less all-pervasive than previously.

In approaching this question, seems safe to start with axiom that Soviets strongly opposed to seeing West Germany firmly allied to West, and even more so to seeing a united Germany in this position, that on contrary they very much want a united Germany brought into Commie orbit, and that they greatly prefer achieve this aim by methods short of war. Corollary follows that Soviets presumably really do want united Germany, but only if can get on own terms, and if terms good enough to compensate for loosening control on Soviet Zone.

In consequence, seems probable that Soviets would decide to retire from East Germany, if at all, only if induced to make such decision through one or both of following considerations.

A. That integration of West Germany with Western Europe, and its progressive rearmament, represents serious threat to Soviet expansion and possibly eventually to Soviet security; and that process in question can only be stopped by agreement providing for some kind of "neutralization" of a united Germany, and withdrawal of US and West European forces behind Germany's borders.

B. That withdrawal of both East and West from unified Germany would later be followed by gradual integration of all Germany into Commie orbit, presumably through utilization of time-tested (and to date generally successful) techniques of Commie penetration, highly organized use of propaganda, subversion, manipulation of "mass organizations," etc. In Germany, may be assumed that some reliance might also be placed on fact of naturally complementary economies of Germany and East Europe, and on historical attraction of authoritarian forms of government for German people.

Events in recent weeks have possibly somewhat strengthened consideration paragraph A. Progress toward Western European integration must to some degree have increased apprehension and effect is showing in acceleration of drive for peace treaty. As to paragraph B, confidence of Kremlin in achieving result outlined, under given conditions, cannot be judged accurately. Must be frankly admitted that we do not (repeat not) at present know just how far Soviets would go to reach agreement. But intensity of current peace treaty campaign suggests possibility they might desire same on any terms where they would consider chances appreciably better than 50-50 of eventual absorption of all Germany.

In this connection true that short-term effects of withdrawal could have undesirable repercussions in satellites, from Soviet point view, which doubtless affects calculations and makes offering concessions less attractive. Yet Kremlin's record shows considerable predilection for long-range planning.

Problem thus becomes one of estimating how much Soviets might concede, and still think, that long-term odds in their favor and short-term disadvantages outweigh thereby.

Comparison of Soviet note and current propaganda line with earlier Soviet and DDR [Deutsche Demokratische Republik, or German Democratic Republic] approaches to problems seems to indicate that present approach, if looked at from strict reading of note's text, contains less that could block agreement, and that perhaps somewhat more conciliatory tone appears on surface. Some clue might also be found in relatively inoffensively worded but still obvious attempts to stack cards for possibly forthcoming discussions in own favor, as found in text of Soviet note; e.g., suggested participants; emphasis on speed, talk of "democratic" principles; maintenance of troops in Germany for year after treaty signed or having a provision for reprisals against "non-cooperative" Germans. Soviets may feel that, given advantages which could be derived from implementation of such jokers, their position would be favorable enough to risk an agreement involving mutual withdrawal from Germany.

Nevertheless, despite above, no convincing evidence to date that maximum Soviet concessions will in fact reach point where West could accept. One informed German observer even stated that Soviet provisions so cleverly worded to bring all things to all men, that could not (repeat not) be genuine. Probability exists that only bargaining process itself, if discussions undertaken, could give complete answer, although Commie attitude toward UN Commission in Germany, Austrian treaty, and future Soviet reactions toward West's proposals regarding German elections may give some hints. Continuing analysis will be attempted, and additional considerations submitted as available.

In any event, even though Soviets presumably hope for agreement on own minimum terms, they can hardly feel assurance that this will result and it must be assumed plans already worked out for procedure in rather likely event that offer of discussions turned down by West, or discussions commenced and then break down. Estimate of alternative Soviet program will be subject of separate telegram.

DOCUMENT FOUR

TELEGRAM FROM PHILIP BONSAL TO DEAN ACHESON
March 15, 1952

[Jacquin de] Margerie discussed Sov[iet] note with me briefly this morning. He stated that one must interpret any Sov[iet] move in light numerous possible objectives and that fact some of these inconsistent with others not sufficient reason for not taking all of them into account. Because of Sov[iet] conviction time is on their side and against capitalist west, they feel they can explore fully every avenue of attack, even the most unpromising, and not bother about seeming contradictions.

Recognizing propaganda aspects of recent Sov[iet] move, Margerie said that it may reflect fundamental Sov[iet] political decision, i.e. abandonment of any immediate design of military aggression in W Europe. He believes Sov[iets] may now feel that, primarily because of industrial potential of US and its mobilization for rearmament pur-

SOURCE: DoS 662.001/3-1552. Incoming Telegram No. 5624 from Paris, Secret Security Information.

poses, prospects of successful military adventure in West have become dim and therefore wise course is to allow economic and social strains to pursue their task of preparing W Europe for Communism, with Sov[iet] support of the violent spread of communism (notably by Chinese) being concentrated in Asia.

In light of such decision, he said, Soviet consent to rearmament of Germany becomes explicable in terms of alternatives available to Soviets. One of those is to allow W Germany to proceed on present course of integration with west and of participation in EDC. This possibility, now moving into realm of the highly probable, is most repugnant to Soviet. But they recognize impossibility under present conditions of indefinite disarmament of Germany. Therefore they have proposed that a united Germany not (repeat not) integrated into west or EDC be given limited right to rearm. According to Margerie, they have no illusions as to enforceability of such limitations on armament in case of nation of seventy millions with German characteristics, but they feel that there would at least be good prospect such united Germany would not be entirely on side of west in east-west questions. In fact, maintenance of traditional Franco-German hatreds, suspicions and frictions would over short term be one of results to be anticipated.

If Soviets in fact are thinking in this manner and see any prospects of successful application of their policy, Margerie believes they will eventually consent to some election formula which will result in discard of GDR leaders, with Soviets consoling themselves with thought that alternative would be tightly integrated W Europe including FED-REP [Federal Republic], attraction of which upon E Germany would presumably be irresistible, especially if Soviets had reached decision not to pursue objectives in Europe by overt military methods.

Furthermore, Margerie believes that regardless of ultimate Soviet objectives, main immediate purpose of Soviet move is to delay western integration and to postpone final EDC and contractual decisions. He feels that while we would make reasonably prompt and efficacious reply to Soviet proposals, our major energies should continue to be devoted to surmounting remaining obstacles to conclusion of contractual arrangements and of EDC treaty.

DOCUMENT FIVE

TELEGRAM FROM SIR IVONE KIRKPATRICK TO FOREIGN OFFICE
March 17, 1952

The High Commissioners took an opportunity today to ask the Federal Chancellor for his views.

2. The Chancellor said that he would describe what he did not want. First he was against a Four-Power conference. It would lead to no results, would last too long and would slow up progress towards European Defence Community and the integration of Europe. Secondly he was against a purely negative answer. This would have a bad psychological result in Germany. We must at least examine the possibilities and when drafting the reply, the account should be taken of psychological reactions in Allied countries, particularly in Germany and France, where certain circles are afraid of a German contribution to defence.

3. The Chancellor said that he had been struck by the nationalist tone

SOURCE: PRO, FO 371/97878/C 1074/20 Telegram No. 298, Priority, Confidential.

in parts of the note, such as the references to the Nazis and the generals and the proposal that the Germans should have a national army. He had always considered that movements such as the S.R.P. had no great importance as there was nothing behind them. But if Russia started to support this line then he feared that these movements might gain greater importance.

4. The Chancellor thought that we should try to show up the Russian note by replying with some precise questions which could easily be understood by public opinion in the rest of the world. There were two in particular which should be asked. Firstly, if, as is proposed in the note, the Russians want an all-German government after free elections, are they prepared to let the United Nations Commission into the Soviet Zone to carry out the same investigations which they are now carrying out in the Federal Republic? Secondly, what do the Russians mean when they say that Germany must not enter into alliances with any country which was at war with the Soviet Union? [sic!] Does this include such projects as the Schuman Plan, E.D.C. and the integration of Europe?

5. Finally, the Chancellor said that he did not think there was any need, nor would it be right to raise the question of the Oder-Neisse line. But in order that there should be no misunderstanding he wanted once more to make clear to us his position on this question. No German Government could ever state that it accepted this frontier. He had said before and he still maintained that the solution of the problem must be left to the future and that in the meantime every effort should be made to avoid friction between Germany and Poland so that a later solution would be possible with the minimum difficulty.

6. I referred to the ambiguity in the Russian note over Potsdam and the Oder-Neisse line and I asked the Chancellor if he thought it would be right or wrong to point out in our reply that these frontiers had not been laid down at Potsdam. The Chancellor thought it would be right.

7. Finally, François-Poncet said that whether this Russian note lead to a series of diplomatic exchanges or even a conference, the essential was not to hold up our negotiations. With this all agreed.

DOCUMENT SIX

MINUTES OF A MEETING OF U.S., U.K., FRENCH, AND GERMAN REPRESENTATIVES

March 20, 1952

Mr. Schuman opened the meeting by outlining three points which the Western Powers felt should go into the reply (to the Soviet note of March 10). First, we should say that in order to have a government we must have elections and in this connection we thought it important to stress the role of the UN Commission. Second, we should insist upon the freedom of such a government to carry on its policy in the period between the election and the conclusion of the treaty. Third, the Soviet note had proposed a "schema" for a peace treaty and we ought to respond to some of the points contained therein. He mentioned national forces and restrictions on political liberty (i.e., Germany should not enter any coalition).

Mr. Schuman said that we did not intend to speak of all the questions raised by the Soviets but only a few examples. He asked Chancel-

Source: DoS 662.001/3-2052, Secret, Security Information.

lor Adenauer what the latter considered to be necessary for German public opinion and his own policy.

Mr. Adenauer said he would first like to speak of the psychological situation in Germany. Such nationalistic groups as existed had been without great importance heretofore. They had had no adequate financial support and no support from any strong outside source. These groups were now appealed to by the paragraphs in the Soviet note concerning an army, votes for ex-Nazis, etc. He did not doubt that the Soviet Government was ready to support these groups also with money. It appeared to him that the Soviet Union had modified its policy to one of support for nationalist instead of Communist groups.

He thought the reply to the Soviet note must clarify the situation and take note of these facts. Conversations with the Soviets should be avoided because they would give time for strengthening of the nationalist groups. On the other hand he emphasized that one must avoid treating unification of Germany as something of no great importance. Thirdly, it was absolutely necessary rapidly to complete our policy of integration and defense. This policy was especially necessary in consequence not only of the war but also of Soviet policies. The aim of the West is to guarantee peace. In the fourth place, he felt the reply should make clear that an all-German Government can only be elected under conditions of freedom and that the UN Commission should be treated as a necessary condition to dissipate doubts as to the situation. He expressed the hope that the reply could be sent while the UN Commission was still in Germany and ready to function.

Mr. Adenauer counselled against discussing the functions and powers of the German Government as he felt this problem was too complicated. He advised keeping the answer short and clear. He thought it should include a statement that the Western Allies were ready to follow any promising path to a solution.

Mr. Schuman inquired whether the Chancellor thought the reply should speak of the Potsdam conference, with special reference to frontiers. Mr. Adenauer thought it should only say that the Potsdam decisions were provisional, not definitive. As an additional thought, he suggested that the reply might make the point that no provision against German entry into "coalitions" could be allowed to cut off the plans for European unity—the Schuman Plan, the EDC, etc.

Mr. Eden and Mr. Dunn said they had nothing to ask the Chancellor.

Mr. Adenauer said he wanted especially to say to the French that if they wanted to mention the unacceptable nature of the Soviet provision for a German national army—and he himself did not wish a German national army—that would be all right with him.

Mr. Eden asked when the note should be sent, to which Adenauer replied "as soon as possible."

Mr. Schuman pointed out that we did not wish to give the impression that if we spoke of only one or two questions there were not others to be resolved. Mr. Adenauer felt it was not good from the Germans' standpoint to enter into discussions with the Russians. The note must clearly end these questions. Mr. Schuman thought that if we spoke only of elections and the Russians should accept we should be led immediately into discussions.

Mr. Adenauer suggested in conclusion that if we waited four or five days to send the note the UN Commission would have repeated its request for entry into the Soviet Zone and he thought the time of the note should be coordinated with the actions of the UN Commission.

DOCUMENT SEVEN

MEMORANDUM OF JOHN FERGUSON, POLICY PLANNING STAFF
March 27, 1952

1. The reply of the three Western Powers has now been delivered in Moscow, and various press statements have been issued in the three Western capitals.

2. The probability is that the Russian rejoinder will make the following main points:

a. The Western Powers will be charged with obstructing a German peace treaty, preventing the unification of Germany, and preparing a new war.
b. The UN will be held to be without competence in German matters.
c. The question of all-German elections will be regarded as one primarily concerning the Germans themselves, with appropriate four power supervision.

SOURCE: DoS 662.001/3-2752, Top Secret, Security Information.

   d. Representatives of the GDR and the Federal Republic should work out the arrangements for all-German elections and discussions to this end should be promptly initiated.

   e. The four powers having responsibility for Germany should initiate discussions of a German peace treaty at an early specified date, say April 30.

3. A Russian rejoinder along these lines would probably not cause us much trouble. The West Germans are quite sophisticated in these matters and are unlikely to be misled by proposals which are unaccompanied by solid evidences of a change in Soviet policy in East Germany. An actual relaxation of controls in East Germany would, it is believed, be necessary to produce an impact on West German opinion sufficient to delay or block progress on the EDC. U.S. intelligence agencies estimate that the Russians are not prepared to pay such a price to affect developments in the West. We shall probably be able, therefore, to proceed with our present policies without much trouble.

4. However, we cannot be sure that this estimate is correct and we should prepare to deal with a change in Russian policy. There is a possibility that the Russians are prepared to pay some price to delay or block progress on the EDC. There is also a possibility that West German support for EDC can be undermined by measures which, though involving some political disadvantages for the Russians, would not really endanger the East German regime or the Russian position in East Germany. The Russians may attempt, in a series of exchanges, to delay or block progress on the EDC at the smallest possible cost, upping their bid each time until they either achieve success or decide that the price is too high.

5. There are a number of actions which the Russians could take, ranging from hollow, verbal concessions to the holding of free elections. As has been pointed out, proposals unaccompanied by solid evidences of a change in Soviet policy will probably not cause us much trouble. What we should be on the lookout for are actions or proposals involving a pledge of action subject to the initiation of discussions. In rough order of cost to the Russians, such actions might include:

   a. Invitations might be issued to prominent West German political leaders to speak freely in East Germany, accompanied or followed by proposals that representatives of the GDR and the FDR [Federal Republic of Germany] investigate conditions in East and West and subsequently arrange all-German elections.

b. The SPD and perhaps other parties in East Germany might be licensed—on a controlled and phoney basis but with enough hullabaloo to give an appearance of a revival of party politics in East Germany.

c. The foregoing actions might be taken and combined with other actions designed to show that the conditions necessary for all-German elections now exist and to set the stage for meetings between East and West Germans "to work things out." The GDR might pass an all-German election law resembling the West German law in all but a few key points which, it could be said, could be ironed out in negotiations. The GDR might hold elections to an "all-German" constituent assembly on the basis of this law and suggest that the West Germans do the same.

d. All-Berlin elections under quadripartite supervision might be proposed—on the theory that the communist government of the East Berlin sector would be a sufficient burnt offering to demonstrate the possibilities of all-German elections and that the basic Soviet interests in East Berlin could be protected by the Soviet troops.

e. A conference with the Western Powers to discuss the Eastern boundaries of Germany might be proposed—on the basis that the Russians had assumed that there was agreement on the Potsdam decision and that, in view of the Western reply, this topic ought to be re-examined. Indications might be given of an intention to return certain territories to Germany (with Poland to be compensated elsewhere).

f. The position on the UN investigating commission might be reversed—on the theory that a Potemkin village affair might be staged and the commission sufficiently confused to write an inconclusive report. It is unlikely that this move would be taken, however, unless the Russians had decided to proceed with free elections. (This move might fit well with other Russian moves in other parts of the world, such as an effort to bring the Korean matter into the Security Council, and a general effort to improve the Russian position in the UN.)

g. The position on the UN investigating commission might be maintained and countered by a proposal that a four power investigating group should be set up and that simultaneously discussions to prepare an election should be initiated. The Russians probably would feel unable to take this step unless they had decided to proceed with free elections, but they might feel that these elections could be delayed for a long time. It is possible that they might feel that the movement toward free elections could be halted at any time and the situation sufficiently confused by charges about conditions in West Germany to avoid a heavy political cost.

h. Finally, the Russians might at some time decide actually to proceed with free elections and to the creation, as a matter of policy, of an Austrian-type situation in Germany.

6. From the Russian point of view, the difficulty with taking any steps of this kind, even the least costly, is that the step or steps would involve a political price and would be exposed as phoney unless the Russians were eventually willing to go all the way to free elections. If they were exposed, progress on EDC could be resumed with greater speed and resolve then if the Russians had not once more revealed by their actions that German unity is not a real alternative to the integration of Western Germany into Western Europe. For this reason, it is believed the Russians will probably not take any big steps toward free elections unless they are prepared to go all the way to an Austrian-type situation.

7. Even the least of the steps listed above would probably have sufficient impact on West German opinion to block progress on EDC temporarily. If the Russian rejoinder to our reply involved action pointing toward free elections, we will have to give more weight than we now do to the possibility that there has been a change in Russian policy. And we should consider now how we might best deal with a move toward free elections by the Russians. It would still be an important aim to conclude, if possible, the contractual arrangements and the signing of the EDC—for to get these out of the way would improve either our ability to proceed without delay once the phoneyness of the Russian move had been exposed or our bargaining position with the Russians once we had found out that their tactic was to up their bids as necessary to block EDC. In the event that Russian policy has changed, we want to make them pay as high a price as possible since we will be forced to give up a line of development in which we have a large investment.

8. If the second Russian note suggests that this may be our problem, S/P believes that the second Western note should seek to compel the Russians either to abandon their game or to go quickly all the way to free elections. It is recognized that it will be difficult to draft a note which will compel the Russians to make such a choice and perhaps even more difficult to sell it to our allies. The Russians are skilled in countering so as to avoid commitments and to escape responsibility for

obstruction. Their skill is supported by the tendency of our allies to believe that any and every Russian proposal should be thoroughly explored in such a way as to avoid giving any offense to the Russians. Nevertheless, the effort to draft such a note and to prepare our allies for the possible need for such a note is believed worthwhile.

9. A note of this kind would probably take the Russians by surprise. It should bring home to them that the unification game, if it is to be played at all, will be played seriously and to a conclusion. If the Russians have doubts about the wisdom of moving toward free elections and have merely made, in their second note, an exploratory move to test the solidity of Western opinion, such a note might precipitate a firm Russian decision one way or the other. There is a possibility that enough time would be required to make their decision and to plan their next move to enable us to conclude the contractual arrangements and the signing of the EDC. Even if we could not complete these actions before their rejoinder, we would by such a note maximize the chance of obtaining a refusal which would enable us to proceed with present policies and also improve our ability to exploit a Russian acceptance to our advantage. These advantages, it is believed, outweigh the advantages of a second Western reply which would merely reiterate, with appropriate modifications, the views expressed in the first Western note and which would give the Russians a better opportunity for blocking present Western policies at a small cost.

DOCUMENT EIGHT

TELEGRAM FROM JOHN McCLOY
TO DEAN ACHESON
March 29, 1952

I. Not (repeat not) without good reason Germans are strongly inclined to view Soviet note of March 10 as addressed to them rather than to the Allies. They therefore tend to examine it as a serious offer of unity rather than as a propaganda move.

It is particularly difficult to judge German public opinion so soon after exchange of notes but we tend to believe that Germans' experiences of Russia as occupiers, prisoners of war and occupied make them skeptical of any Soviet offer and that are therefore not (repeat not) as yet greatly impressed by it. This negative reaction is, however, not (repeat not) static and may be reversed by the politicians particularly if West Powers appear to oppose unification.

Among those politicians who have carefully studied implications of note and our reply there are basically two schools of thought. Adenauer

SOURCE: DoS 662.001/3-2952. Incoming Telegram No. 2188 from Bonn, Priority, Secret.

whose entire political creed is based on Western integration considers note chiefly an effort to disrupt his policy. Some of his advisors intimately familiar with Russia hold to view that Kremlin is in dead earnest in its intention not (repeat not) only of disrupting integration but of reorienting Germany to the East with initial status perhaps more like Finland or even Sweden than Czechoslovakia but eventually as a junior partner in Soviet drive for world domination. They see a parallel between situation today and in 1939 when Westerners were futilely negotiating with Russians to prevent a German-Russia alliance which was so rudely shattered by Stalin's dramatic offer to Hitler resulting in Molotov Ribbentropp Act. Aware of challenge of such an offer Adenauer firmly believes it is up to Germany to prove her loyalty to West by rejecting it flatly and expediting conclusion of Defence Treaty and contractuals.

Adenauer however is constrained by fact that flat rejection gives appearance of forsaking Germany's own national interests in interests of Western Europe or as one Cabinet member put it of being more American than the Americans.

Coalition elements less wedded to European integration as an end in itself, more sensitive to charges of Quislingism and more susceptible to nationalist slogans oppose flat rejection and urge further exploration of Soviet offer before final commitment to West. This group recommends a slowing down rather than speeding up of current negotiations. Thus far it is not (repeat not) very strong comprising chiefly a few softheaded nationalists like Bleucher, and some left-wing CDU including Kaiser *and Brentano*. However, as connection between integration and unification be, is clearer especially after Allied notes stressed connection and as time for ratification draws closer, we can envisage strengthening of this school and growing reluctance to take final step that might be construed by public as slamming door on unification unless in meantime it is made absolutely clear to Germans that Soviet offer of unification is unacceptable to them. With Soviet offer opening apparently new vista, however bogus, some deputies may also be tempted to be more critical in their scrutiny of the terms of integration as contained in the contractual agreement.

Basically SPD is through the long experience less sensitive to Soviet blandishments than possibly less experienced elements in coalition. However, because of its stubborn policy of opposition to Adenauer and especially to his policy of integration it may very well be tempted to side with the temporizers in coalition. Herefore it has been possible to maintain at least semblance of unity between opposition and Government on East-West problems, but with evidence of difference of opinion within coalition itself it may prove difficult to hold SPD in line on this major issue.

II. German reactions to specific points of Soviet proposal are difficult to define but some general observation may be pertinent.

(A) Oder-Neisse Line is, of course, *least palatable of Soviet proposals.* Initially Germans were inclined to *view that* no (repeat no) German Government could accept settlement which did not (repeat not) involve return of east provinces. However, some Germans are now (repeat now) veering to view that they should take what they can get today and wait for rest till a more favorable opportunity arises.

(B) National Army. To many Germans, Soviet offer of national army has attraction of forbidden fruit as Allies had only offered participation in strange new concept of European Defence Force. In view of widespread fear of a return of the old militarism, this may appear irrational but there is no (repeat no) doubt that in many quarters Soviet offer has had a real appeal based on nationalism and the traditions and emotions connected with a German national army.

(C) Freedom of alliances. [Helene] Wessel's and Heinemann's neutrality doctrines have attracted far more attention than support in Germany. Nevertheless, if unification on acceptable terms appeared genuinely purchaseable at price of provisional neutralization, many Germans might be tempted to consider deal in belief that once reunited Germany would be strong enough to regain her freedom to choose her allies.

(D) Freedom of trade. This Soviet proposal would seem to be particularly attractive to German industry. As yet we have no (repeat no) concrete evidence of the Ruhr's reaction to Soviet note or our reply. However there are just enough straws in wind indicating Adenauer's industrial supporters are urging him to go slow on the contractual negotiations, to prompt us to investigate this interesting phase more carefully. We believe for example that Bluecher's adherence to Kaiser school may be prompted by Dusseldorf's covetousness of Eastern markets particularly in event of business recession.

III. Thus far practical political result of exchange of notes has been a tendency in some circles to take another look at Western integration, particularly its possible incompatibility with unification, and there is a small but growing group who are urging Adenauer to go slow. Vigorously opposing them, Adenauer remains insistent on a speedy conclusion of agreements. Thus far he has behind him a majority of the

Cabinet and the tacit support of a majority of the coalition and probably also a large portion of the electorate.

Nevertheless we cannot (repeat not) afford to disregard potentialities of those who would delay agreements pending clarification of Soviet intentions, particularly if there is evidence of a similar trend in either France or UK. They have cheap but powerful nationalistic slogans and can make popular charge that Adenauer is dividing Germany's loyalties between her Eastern provinces and the West. Furthermore they have in the Saar issue an instrument of considerable tactical force to bring pressure on Adenauer to go slowly by demanding that the Saar problem be solved before any further commitments are made to West.

DOCUMENT NINE

TELEGRAM FROM
SIR IVONE KIRKPATRICK
TO FOREIGN OFFICE
April 16, 1952

At discussion with Chancellor this afternoon he said he would like to add two points to those he had made to me last Friday.

2. He suggested that in replying we should enquire whether the exclusion of a United Germany from any coalitions, on which the Russians insisted, meant for instance its exclusion from the European Defence Community and the Schuman Plan. No doubt it did: but it would be well to force the Russians to say so. Too many simpletons in Germany would find some specious attractions in the Soviet Note until it could be shown in concrete terms what it meant.

3. The Russians had now proposed a Four-Power commission to enquire into conditions for holding all-German elections. He had already explained last Friday the importance he attached to the United Nations

SOURCE: PRO, FO 371/97881/C 1074/81. Telegram No. 380, Priority, Confidential.

commission. But perhaps our reply to the Russian note could ask them specifically whether, whatever commission might make the enquire, they would be prepared, should it find by a majority that conditions in the Russian zone made free elections impossible, to modify those conditions so as to make them comply with what the commission regarded as essential for free elections.

4. The Chancellor added there was a risk of the public as a whole getting the impression that the initiative and the more generous policy were on the Soviet side. They appeared to be offering something constructive; we must not appear merely to be turning it down in a negative and obstructive way. Let us therefore take the offensive in our reply, put some colour in it, and show on which side freedom lay.

5. I shall report by saving telegram tomorrow certain less important observations by the Chancellor and some interesting ones by McCloy and François-Poncet.

TELEGRAM FROM JOHN McCLOY
TO DEAN ACHESON
May 3, 1952

Chancellor told me today that after serious consideration yesterday and "through half the night," he had definitely concluded US proposal for meeting in Berlin (paragraph 9 Department's telegram 2850) would be a mistake at this time. If meeting is now (repeat now) suggested, Chancellor doubts that Cabinet would authorize him to sign contractual agreements until meeting had demonstrated whether Soviets sincere in their offer of free elections. He would expect opposition to insist that meetings take place before signature, but now (repeat now) fears even members of Government would take same line. He also believes it would be unwise to limit any quadripartite meeting to discussion of free election issue as Soviets might be prepared to make sufficient concessions to justify lengthy negotiations. During course of these, public attention would be concentrated on the concessions and tend to

SOURCE: DoS 662.001/5-352. Incoming Telegram no. 2649 from Bonn, Priority, Secret.

overlook other objectionable phases of Soviet proposal. In these circumstances it would be impossible to conclude defence negotiations.

His view of the tactics to pursue are as follows:

(1) HICOMers [High Commissioners] should immediately write [W. I.] Chuikov asking for answer to their earlier communications on free elections which remain unanswered.

(2) Allied reply to Soviet note should pose series questions such as "what rights do Soviets contemplate new government would possess?" and "what rights would new government have in respect of Schuman Plan, EDC, etc?" Allied note should also include general statement of Allied objectives and reasons for them to be contrasted with Soviet proposal for German National Army.

Chancellor believes (1) above would be very good way to stress Allied interest in free elections and in Bundestag conditions for them. If Chuikov's answer should come in before despatch of Allied reply to Soviet note, it could be dealt with in that reply and if not (repeat not) as seems more likely, failure to answer could be referred to. Adenauer believes this would be sufficient to satisfy German public opinion and would avoid heavy risks of delaying signature of agreements which is now (repeat now) entailed in proposal for early meeting.

My own view is that his suggestion of a series of questions would appear too much like fencing and thus lose public support. Can see no (repeat no) harm in HICOM prodding Chuikov but I do not (repeat not) believe it would carry much weight with German public opinion.

As radio reports from Paris today disclosed existence of US proposal, I felt free to mention it to [Ernst] *Reuter* who after weighing disadvantages and possible benefits said that on balance he would favor meeting but full exploration of the hazards of such action was not (repeat not) made with him.

In telephone conversation with London this afternoon, we understand US proposal has been modified in tripartite discussions and substitute is being offered on which we will comment as soon as received.

NOTES

Preface

1. Rolf Steininger, *Eine Chance zur Wiedervereinigung? Darstellung und Dokumentation auf der Grundlage unveröffentlichter britischer und amerikanischer Akten*, Beiheft 12 des Archivs für Sozialgeschichte (Bonn, 1985). A second edition appeared in 1986, a third in 1990. A paperback edition of the introduction appeared as *Eine vertane Chance: Die Stalin-Note vom 10. März 1952 und die Wiedervereinigung* (Bonn, 1985).

2. This assumption was substantiated by Dean Acheson, the American secretary of state, who referred to the great participation of the British in his memoirs, *Present at the Creation* (New York, 1969), pp. 630f.

1. The Stalin Note and German Scholarship

1. "Draft of Soviet Government of Peace Treaty with Germany," *Department of State Bulletin* (April 7, 1952), 26:532; and *FRUS 1952–1954*, vol. 7,

1. The Stalin Note

Document No. 65. The Stalin Note was sent by the Soviet government to the governments of Great Britain, France, and the United States.

2. Hans-Peter Schwarz, ed., *Die Legende von der verpaßten Gelegenheit: Die Stalin-Note vom 10. März 1952*, vol. 5 of *Rhöndorfer Gespräche* (Stuttgart, 1982), p. 13. (Hereafter cited as *Rhöndorfer Gespräche* 5). The title of this conference publication—literally "The Legend of the Missed Opportunity"— suggests a conclusion that only partially agrees with the contributed articles, especially those of the contemporary witnesses.

3. *Rhöndorfer Gespräche* 5:82.

4. Paul Sethe, *Zwischen Bonn und Moskau* (Frankfurt, 1956).

5. Deutscher Bundestag, Stenograph. Berichte, 3. *Wahlperiode, 9. Sitzung*, pp. 297–419.

6. As Wilhelm Grewe put it in the *Frankfurter Allgemeine Zeitung*, March 10, 1982.

7. Konrad Adenauer, *Erinnerungen* (Stuttgart, 1960), 2:265.

8. Carlo Schmid, *Erinnerungen* (Bern, 1979), p. 527.

9. Hans Buchheim, "Die Legende von der verpaßten Gelegenheit," *Frankfurter Allgemeine Zeitung*, April 15, 1969; Jürgen Weber, "Das sowjetische Wiedervereinigungsangebot," *Aus Politik und Zeitgeschichte* (1969), no. 50; the controversy between G. W. Zickenheimer and J. Weber in *Aus Politik und Zeitgeschichte* (1970), 40:35–40; Wolfgang Wagner, "Wiedervereinigung Modell 1952: Der Versuch einer Legendenbildung in der deutschen Innenpolitik," *Wort und Wahrheit* (1958), 13:175ff.; Gerhard Wettig, "Der publizistische Appell als Kampfmittel: Die sowjetische Deutschland-Kampagne vom Frühjahr 1952," in his *Politik im Rampenlicht* (Frankfurt, 1967), pp. 136–184. Wettig strengthens his position in his newest article: "Wiedervereinigungsangebot oder Propagandaaktion," *Deutschland Archiv* (1982), 2:130–148, as does Hans Buchheim, *Deutschlandpolitik 1949–1972: Der politisch-diplomatische Prozeß* (Stuttgart, 1984), pp. 56–65. Buchheim not only engages in polemics but also ignores the most recent literature on the subject, and he speaks of "wishful thinking as suspiciousness": "Here are the people who do not want to accept reality; here arise the myths of individuals' biographies as well as of the history of a nation and its people" (p. 65).

10. Boris Meissner, *Rußland, die Westmächte und Deutschland: Die sowjetische Deutschland-Politik 1943–1953* (Hamburg, 1953; 2d ed., 1954); Boris Meissner, "Die Sowjetunion und die deutsch Frage 1949–1955," in Dietrich Geyer, ed., *Sowjetunion: Außenpolitik 1917–1955* (Cologne, 1972), pp. 449–501.

11. Richard Löwenthal, *Vom Kalten Krieg zur Ostpolitik* (Stuttgart, 1974), pp. 17f., and in the introduction to Arnulf Baring's, *Der 17. Juni 1953* (Stuttgart, 1983).

12. Klaus Erdmenger, *Das folgenschwere Mißverständis: Bonn und die sowjetische Deutschlandpolitik 1949–1955* (Freiburg, 1967); Gerd Meyer, *Die sowjetische Deutschland-Politik im Jahre 1952* (Tübingen, 1970).

13. "Träume vom Deutschen Reich," *Die Zeit*, October 12, 1984.

14. Andreas Hillgruber, "Adenauer und die Stalin-Note vom März 1952," in Dieter Blumenwitz et al., eds., *Konrad Adenauer und seine Zeit*, vol. 2 of *Beiträge der Wissenschaft* (Stuttgart, 1976), pp. 125–126. In his interesting article entitled "Das Deutschlandbild und die Deutschlandpolitik Josef Stalins" in *Deutschland Archiv* (1979) 12:1258–1282, Wolfgang Pfeiler stresses: "The seriousness of this diplomatic campaign was politically coordinated. This can be seen in the use of political language: under Stalin, Malenkov, Beria, and Suslov, all statements about Germany were differentiated to indicate whether one was speaking of the present or the future. For the present, the terms 'West Germany' and 'GDR' were used; for the future, only the term 'Germany.' Also, maps printed in Omsk in 1952 do not indicate the borders of the zones and only carry the designation 'Germany,' but even then Germany ran only as far as the Oder–Neisse line. In an interview on March 31, 1952, the authenticity of the diplomatic note from Stalin was personally verified; in addition, the May Day slogans of 1952 gave a priority to settling the status of Germany that this issue had never had before nor would ever have again" (p. 1280).

15. Hermann Graml, "Nationalstaat oder westdeutscher Teilstaat: Die sowjetische Noten vom Jahre 1952 und die öffentliche Meinung in der Bundesrepublik Deutschland," *Vierteljahrshefte für Zeitgeschichte* (1977), 25:821–864.

16. Hermann Graml, "Die Legende von der verpaßten Gelegenheit: Zur sowjetischen Notenkampagne des Jahres 1952," *Vierteljahrshefte für Zeitgeschichte* (1981), 29:340–341.

17. *Rhöndorfer Gespräche* 5:52ff. (Gerstenmaier), 47 (Gradl), 67 (Thomas).

18. Ibid., 58ff. Ulbricht's speech was reprinted on June 10, 1960, in *Neues Deutschland*, and it is also in *Dokumente zur Deutschland-Politik: 4. Reihe*, p. 1134.

19. *Rhöndorfer Gespräche* 5:62.

20. Ibid.

21. Ibid., pp. 74, 82, 89.

22. "Ein zählebiger Mythos: Stalins Note vom März 1952. Der Irrtum über die 'verpaßte Gelegenheit' zu einer deutschen Wiedervereinigung," *Frankfurter Allgemeine Zeitung*, March 10, 1982. Wilhelm Grewe, born in 1911, was a close political adviser to Konrad Adenauer after 1951. Initially, he led the German delegation at the negotiations concerning the cancellation of the Occupation Statute. Later, he played a substantial role in working out the European Defense Community Treaty and the Paris Treaties in October 1954; together with Herbert Blankenhorn, he led the Federal Republic's observer delegation to the four-power foreign ministers' conference in Berlin in January and February 1954; he also attended the foreign ministers' conference in Geneva in 1959. Then, until he retired, he served as ambassador to Washington, NATO, and Tokyo.

23. *Rhöndorfer Gespräche* 5:54f.

24. "Ein zählebiger Mythos," *Frankfurter Allgemeine Zeitung*, March 10, 1982.

25. Canadian embassy in Moscow to Foreign Minister Lester Pearson in Ottawa, July 26, 1952. PRO, FO 371/97850/C 10144/28, Secret.

26. Rolf Steininger, *Deutsche Geschichte 1945–1961: Darstellung und Dokumente in zwei Bänden* (Frankfurt, 1983; 5th ed., 1989), pp. 410f., as well as my contribution in Josef Foschepoth, ed., *Kalter Krieg und Deutsche Frage: Deutschland im Widerstreit der Mächte 1945–1952* (Göttingen, 1985), pp. 362–379.

27. "Verpaßte Chancen für die Abwendung unserer Teilung?" *Die Zeit,* April 20, 1984.

28. The diary reads: "Nenni asked what role Germany would play in the general international situation. Stalin replied that the rearmament of West Germany would create serious problems; however, (West) Germany was less bellicose than the Americans believed. Moreover, West Germany would have to contend not only with East Germany but also with the Soviet Union, if it should come to a war; the Germans had learned what that meant." Dr. Gerd Bucerius generously provided a translation from the Italian for the author.

29. "Nenni and Stalin," *The New Statesman and Nation,* September 22, 1952.

30. "Verpaßte Chancen für die Abwendung unserer Teilung?" *Die Zeit,* April 20, 1984.

31. The discussion between Stalin and Nenni is said to have played a role in the debate concerning ratification of the treaties with the West. On March 28, 1953, *Die Zeit* published an editorial that caused quite a stir. In this editorial, entitled "Auf krummen Wegen: Geheimabmachung über die endgültige Spaltung Deutschlands," Paul Bourdin, the former federal press secretary, reported that a high-ranking Western diplomat had reminded Kingsbury Smith, the internationally respected director the the International News Service and Adenauer's treasured interviewer, of the Nenni–Stalin discussion. The editorial continued: "Immediately after his discussion with Stalin, Nenni sought out the Italian ambassador in Moscow, Baron Mario di Stefano, and reported to him that Stalin considered any further diplomatic exchange of views with the Western powers concerning Germany merely 'a casual propagandistic measure,' since he believed that it had become impossible to prevent the permanent division of Germany into two states. Therefore, it would be necessary to replace 'the formula of a reunified Germany' with the new concept of two completely separate German states that would develop as 'military and ideologic counterpoints to one another.' " For the controversy surrounding this article, see Arnulf Baring, *Außenpolitik in Adenauers Kanzlerdemokratie* (Munich, 1969), 2:243–250. Joseph and Steward Alsop also spoke to Nenni in August 1952 and published their interview in the *New York Herald Tribune;* it corresponds to the remarks made above. Herbert Blankenhorn, *Verständnis und Verständigung: Blätter eines politischen Tagebuches 1949–1979* (Berlin, 1980), p. 136, refers to the Alsops' interview under the date August 12, 1952.

32. "Rebuilding the Republic," *Times Literary Supplement,* August 17, 1984, p. 921. In this article, Laqueur discusses my book *Deutsche Geschichte.*

33. Graml, "Die Legende von der verpaßten Gelegenheit," p. 333.
34. J. Daridan in Washington to the Quai d'Orsay, June 28, 1952. MAE/Série EU 1949–1955 Allemagne, Série 4, Soussérie 16, Dossier 6: URSS–Allemagne, 1 April 1952–31 March 1953. Telegram No. 4572/79, Secret.
35. "Verpaßte Chancen für die Abwendung unserer Teilung?" *Die Zeit*, April 20, 1984.
36. Bucerius made this assertion in a letter written to the author, February 16, 1984, as well as to Wilhelm Grewe in a program entitled "Zeugen des Jahrhunderts" broadcast on the Second German Television (ZDF) network on December 19, 1983.
37. Letter from G. Kennan to G. Bucerius, December 2, 1972. This correspondence was generously provided by Bucerius.
38. "Verpaßte Chancen für die Abwendung unserer Teilung?" *Die Zeit*, April 20, 1984. This article was based on Countess Dönhoff's letter to Bucerius, August 26, 1973, generously provided by Bucerius.
39. See chapter 8; G. F. Kennan in Moscow to D. Acheson, August 27, 1952. DoS 662.001/8-2752. Incoming Telegram No. 378 from Moscow, Secret. *FRUS 1952–1954*, vol. 7, Document No. 128.
40. Wilfried Loth, *Die Teilung der Welt 1945–1955* (Munich, 1980), p. 287.
41. Especially Weber, "Das sowjetische Wiedervereinigungsangebot," pp. 13f., 22ff.; G. A. Bürger, *Die Legende von 1952: Zur sowjetischen Märznote und ihrer Rolle in der Nachkriegspolitik* (Celle, 1959); Wettig, "Der publizistische Appell als Kampfmittel"; also, Wilhelm Grewe, *Rückblenden 1976–1951: Aufzeichnungen eines Augenzeugen deutscher Außenpolitik von Adenauer bis Schmidt* (Frankfurt, 1979), pp. 412f., refers specifically to communist terminology.
42. As quoted in Gerhard Wettig, *Politik im Rampenlicht*, pp. 156f.
43. "Träume vom Deutschen Reich," *Die Zeit*, October 12, 1984.
44. P. Bonsal in Paris to D. Acheson, March 14, 1952. DoS 662.001/3-1452. Incoming Telegram No. 5602 from Paris, Confidential.
45. S. Reber in Bonn to D. Acheson, June 2, 1952. DoS 662.001/6-252. Incoming Telegram No. 3182 from Bonn, Priority, Secret.
46. G. F. Kennan in Moscow to D. Acheson, May 25, 1952. DoS 662.001/5-2552. Incoming Telegram No. 1881 from Moscow, Secret.
47. S. Reber in Bonn to D. Acheson, June 2, 1952. DoS 662.001/6-252. Incoming Telegram No. 3182 from Bonn, Priority, Secret.

2. The First Soviet Note, March 10, 1952

1. Wilhelm Grewe, in *Frankfurter Allgemeine Zeitung*, March 10, 1982; see also Hans-Peter Schwarz, ed., *Rhöndorfer Gespräche* (Stuttgart, 1982), 5:41f.
2. Theodor Schieder, *Handbuch der europäischen Geschichte* (Stuttgart, 1979), 7:341.
3. Much has been written about this; here I will mention only a few works. First, the classical study by Arnulf Baring, *Außenpolitik in Adenauers Kanzler-*

demokratie (Munich, 1969); Waldemar Besson, *Die Außenpolitik der Bundesrepublik* (Munich, 1970); Paul Noack, *Die Außenpolitik der Bundesrepublik Deutschland*, 2d ed. (Stuttgart, 1981); contributions in the collection of articles by Richard Löwenthal and Hans-Peter Schwarz, eds., *Die zweite Republik: 25 Jahre Bundesrepublik Deutschland: Eine Bilanz* (Stuttgart, 1974; 3d ed., 1979); Dieter Blumenwitz et al., eds., *Konrad Adenauer und seine Zeit: Politik und Persönlichkeit des ersten Bundeskanzlers*, vol. 2 of *Beiträge der Wissenschaft* (Stuttgart, 1976); *Konrad Adenauer. Seine Deutschland- und Außenpolitik 1945–1963* (Munich, 1975), especially the chapters by Rudolf Morsey, "Der politische Aufstieg Konrad Adenauers 1945–1949," Hans-Peter Schwarz, "Das außenpolitische Konzept Konrad Adenauers," and Klaus Gotto, "Adenauers Deutschland- und Ostpolitik 1954–1963"; and finally, Hans-Peter Schwarz, *Die Ära Adenauer 1949–1957*, vol. 2 of *Geschichte der Bundesrepublik Deutschland* (Stuttgart, 1981). In nearly all of these works, the Stalin Note receives a lot of attention. Schwarz in *Die Ära Adenauer* pays less attention to the problems connected with the note. Concerning Adenauer's fundamental decision, see Andreas Hillgruber's penetrating analysis based on Adenauer's *Erinnerungen* and his statements at the time (Andreas Hillgruber, "Adenauer und die Stalin-Note vom März 1952," in Blumenwitz et al., *Konrad Adenauer und seine Zeit* 2:111–130).

4. See Peter Berglar, *Konrad Adenauer: Konkursverwalter oder Erneuerer der Nation?* (Göttingen, 1975), p. 102, quoted in Hillgruber, "Adenauer und die Stalin-Note vom März 1952," p. 124.

5. Baring, *Außenpolitik in Adenauers Kanzlerdemokratie* 1:257.

6. Quoted by Dieter Koch, *Heinemann und die deutsche Frage* (Munich, 1972), p. 324.

7. *Die Welt*, May 14, 1984.

8. Adenauer's speech in *Verhandlungen des Deutschen Bundestages, Stenograph. Berichte, 1. Wahlperiode 1949*, pp. 8095ff. (emphasis added by the author). Parts of the speech are reprinted in Klaus von Schubert, *Sicherheitspolitik der Bundesrepublik Deutschland: Dokumentation 1945–1977* (Cologne, 1978), 1:117ff.

9. *Verhandlungen des Deutschen Bundestages, Stenograph. Berichte, 1. Wahlperiode 1949*, pp. 8108ff.; also in Schubert, *Sicherheitspolitik der Bundesrepublik Deutschland* 1:123ff.

10. *Bulletin des Presse- und Infromationsamtes der Bundesregierung* (March 4, 1952), p. 254.

11. *Bulletin des Presse- und Infromationsamtes der Bundesregierung* (March 6, 1952), p. 262. First quoted by Baring, *Außenpolitik in Adenauers Kanzlerdemokratie* 1:258; also in Hillgruber, "Adenauer und die Stalin-Note vom März 1952," pp. 120f.

12. *Siegener Zeitung*, March 17, 1952, quoted in Hillgruber, "Adenauer und die Stalin-Note vom März 1952," pp. 113f. Unfortunately, the Archiv für Christlich-Demokratische Politik der Konrad-Adenauer-Stiftung does not contain

any documents concerning this speech. (This information was generously provided by the director of the archive, Dr. Klaus Gotto.)

13. Hermann Pünder, *Von Preußen nach Europa: Lebenserinnerungen* (Stuttgart, 1968), p. 488 (stenographic diary entry from March 25, 1952). The entry continues: "As usual, the federal chancellor left immediately following his half-hour talk, since he urgently needed to attend other important meetings. Thus, a discussion in his presence was once again not possible. Many prominent members of our executive committee were not at all pleased by Adenauer's remarks, and the customary polite applause at the conclusion of his talk was remarkably scanty. The people around me—von Brentano, Ernst Lemmer, Ferdinand Friedensburg, Robert Tillmanns, Kiesinger, Paul Bausch, and Bucerius— were united in their criticism."

14. *Rhöndorfer Gespräche* 5:80 and, earlier, in Baring, *Außenpolitik in Adenauers Kanzlerdemokratie* 1:257f.

15. Konrad Adenauer, *Erinnerungen* (Stuttgart, 1966), 1:536.

16. That China certainly did not play such a role as early as 1952 has been pointed out by Hillgruber, "Adenauer und die Stalin-Note vom März 1952," p. 130, among others.

17. Adenauer, *Erinnerungen* 2:87f.

18. Hans Jürgen Küsters, ed., *Adenauer: Teegespräche 1950–1954* (Berlin, 1984).

19. Ibid., p. 332.

20. Ibid., p. 299.

21. Ibid., p. 301.

22. Ibid., p. 477.

23. Ibid., pp. 509, 526.

24. Ibid., p. 259.

25. Ibid., pp. 260, 306, 330.

26. Ibid., p. 260.

27. Ibid.

28. Ibid., p. 308.

29. Ibid., pp. 301, 334, 351, 481, 536.

30. Hillgruber, "Adenauer und die Stalin-Note vom März 1952," p. 125.

31. Küsters, *Adenauer: Teegespräche 1950–1954*, p. 257.

32. Ibid., p. 297.

33. Ibid., p. 297f.

34. Cited by Schwarz, *Die Ära Adenauer* 1:153f., and *Rhöndorfer Gespräche* 5:56. Schwarz relies on the diary of Dr. Lenz, who was then undersecretary in the chancellor's office.

35. I. Kirkpatrick in Wahnerheide to the Foreign Office, March 12, 1952. PRO, FO 371/97877/C 1072/2. Telegram No. 269, from Wahnerheide, Immediate, Confidential, Foreign Office and Whitehall Distribution. Baring, who apparently had the German protocol of this session, quoted Adenauer's decisive first sentence as follows: "The Russian note will not change our policy" (Baring,

Außenpolitik in Adenauers Kanzlerdemokratie 1:255). Also see Grewe in *Rhöndorfer Gespräche* 5:40f.

36. Adenauer, *Erinnerungen* 2:70.

37. Wilhelm Grewe, *Rückblenden 1976–1951: Aufzeichnungen eines Augenzeugen deutscher Außenpolitik von Adenauer bis Schmidt* (Frankfurt, 1979), p. 151; *Rhöndorfer Gespräche* 5:41.

38. *Bulletin des Presse- und Informationsamtes der Bundesregierung* (March 13, 1952), p. 305.

39. Schwarz, *Die Ära Adenauer* 1:155.

40. Kaiser's remarks in *Frankfurter Allgemeine Zeitung*, March 17, 1952, quoted by Baring, *Außenpolitik in Adenauers Kanzlerdemokratie* 1:259 and 2:262.

41. See Koch, *Heinemann und die deutsche Frage*, pp. 32ff.

42. *Verhandlungen des Deutschen Bundestages, Stenograph. Berichte, 1. Wahlperiode 1949, Sitzung am 3./4. 4. 1952*, pp. 8794f.

43. Ibid., pp. 8769, 8777.

44. *Deutschland-Union-Dienst*, March 13, 1952.

3. The Western Powers: Control Through Integration

1. Hans-Peter Schwarz, *Die Ära Adenauer 1949–1957*, vol. 2 of *Geschichte der Bundesrepublik Deutschland* (Stuttgart, 1981), 1:140.

2. Memorandum of the Foreign Office, June 1, 1951. PRO, FO 371/93450/ C 10138. Top Secret.

3. Discussion from January 14, 1952, FO 371/97737.

4. On this point, see Rolf Steininger, *Deutsche Geschichte 1945–1961: Darstellung und Dokumente in zwei Bänden* (Frankfurt, 1983; 5th ed., 1989), p. 24 and chs. 7 and 8.

5. The sentence within parentheses was struck from the original.

6. Excerpt from the note dated May 14, 1948, concerning German unity written by R. M. A. Hankey, head of the northern department in the Foreign Office. PRO, FO 371/70587/C 3653/71/18. Reprinted in Rolf Steininger, "Wie die Teilung Deutschlands verhindert werden sollte: Der Robertson-Plan aus dem Jahre 1948," *Militärgeschichtliche Mitteilungen* (1983), 33:59.

7. Memorandum from Roger Makins, head of the economics section in the Foreign Office, from July 14, 1948. PRO, FO 371/70501/C 5540/3/18, Top Secret. Reprinted in Steininger, "Wie die Teilung Deutschlands verhindert werden sollte," p. 66.

8. Note from Patrick Dean, head of the German section in the Foreign Office, to Christopher Steel, political adviser to the British military governor in Germany, August 10, 1948. PRO, FO 371/70629/C 7068/154/18, Top Secret and Personal. Reprinted in Steininger, "Wie die Teilung Deutschlands verhindert werden sollte," pp. 75–76.

9. Note from Christopher Steel or Patrick Dean, August 16, 1948. PRO, FO

371/70628/C 7043/154/18. Reprinted in Steininger, "Wie die Teilung Deutschlands verhindert werden sollte," pp. 77–78.

10. Note from Sir Ivone Kirkpatrick, Deputy Undersecretary of State in the Foreign Office, September 4, 1948. PRO, FO 371/70628/C 6868/154/18. Reprinted in Steininger, "Wie die Teilung Deutschlands verhindert werden sollte," p. 83.

11. PPS 37, *FRUS 1948* 2:1290.

12. FO 371/70628/C 6868/154.

13. George Marshall on September 21, 1948, at the conference of foreign ministers of the three Western powers held in Paris. *FRUS 1948* 2:1178.

14. Memorandum from Sir Ivone Kirkpatrick, November 25, 1948. PRO, FO 371/70603/C 10710. Reprinted in Steininger, "Wie die Teilung Deutschlands verhindert werden sollte," pp. 83ff.

15. Memorandum by Secretary of State for Foreign Affairs, April 26, 1950. CAB 129/39.

16. Memorandum of the Foreign Office on the future of Germany, April 19, 1950, "The Future of Germany: The Problem of Unity or Division of Germany." PRO, FO 1030/253, Top Secret, PUSC (49) 62 Final Revise, Copy No. 22. On the question of rearmament in December 1950, see Memorandum for Sir William Strang, Foreign Office, for Foreign Minister Ernest Bevin, December 5, 1950, PRO, FO 371/85058/C7955, and Memorandum from Sir Pierson Dixon, Foreign Office, December 9, 1950, PRO, FO 371/85058/C 7955.

17. The *Sovietische Aktiengesellschaften* (SAG) was the designation used by the Soviets in 1946 when they took control of the 200 major German factories in the Eastern occupation zone.

18. Note from Sir Brian Robertson, Wahnerheide, to Sir William Strang, Foreign Office, May 6, 1950. PRO, FO 1030/253, Top Secret and Personal, Copy No. 2.

19. "Draft Statement of German Unity," May 7, 1950, Secret. *FRUS 1950* 3:1088.

20. Waldemar Besson, *Die Außenpolitik der Bundesrepublik: Erfahrungen und Maßstäbe* (Munich, 1979), p. 118.

21. November 29, 1950. PRO, FO 371/85032/C 7372.

22. Bundesministerium für gesamtdeutsche Fragen, ed., *Die Bemühungen der Bundesrepublik um Wiederherstellung der Einheit Deutschlands durch gesamtdeutsche Wahlen*, 4th ed. (Bonn, 1958), pp. 21f.

23. Hugh Dalton's diary entry from December 20, 1950, in Alan Bullock, *Ernest Bevin, Foreign Secretary 1945–1951* (London, 1983), p. 829. This sentence was not printed in Ben Bemlott, ed., *The Political Diary of Hugh Dalton* (London, 1986), p. 495.

24. Memorandum of the Foreign Office, June 1, 1951. PRO, FO 371/93450/C 10138, Top Secret.

25. See I. Kirkpatrick in Wahnerheide to the Foreign Office, September 24 and 25, 1951. PRO, FO 1008/4. Wahnerheide Telegram Nos. 957 and 961, Priority, Confidential; Internal Distribution.

26. Heinrich von Siegler, ed., *Wiedervereinigung und Sicherheit Deutschlands* (Bonn, 1958), pp. 182f.

27. In response to this speech, the representative of the British HIgh Commisssion commented: "It left me with the impression of being the speech of a man who not only does not believe in but was also determined not to have all-German elections. All very splendid so long as the German public did not feel the same way." Note from October 8, 1951. FO 1008/4.

The French ambassador in London, René Massigli, sent the following telegram to the Quai d'Orsay on October 12, 1951:

"One of my coworkers received an interesting response from a Swiss chargé d'affaires who is well acquainted with the Soviet Union and who has maintained contact with Soviet representatives in London. The Soviet diplomats discussed certain topics with him, apparently intending for the information to be repeated even though their words seemingly corresponded to actual tendencies in Russian policy.

"If they are to be believed, Moscow's primary concern is neither the Far nor the Near East, but primarily Germany, which remains a danger for it due to Germany's organizational talent and productivity. Since Moscow fears the reestablishment of an aggressive military power in West Germany and does not believe it can truly rely on East Germany, which is only a source of concern, they would be prepared to abandon East Germany in order to prevent the rearmament of West Germany.

"Thus, *Grotewohl* would be sacrificed, if necessary, but the offer that he negotiated is serious, all the more so because the Russians know that the allies are poorly equipped to oppose their maneuver. Without a doubt this would initially constitute a loss for them, since a united Germany would have every possibility of favoring the West and perhaps joining the Schuman Plan as a united country.

"But if one is to judge by Chancellor Adenauer's failures in public opinion, this Germany would certainly develop toward Social Democracy, with the coexistence of a strong Communist Party. There would thus be a partner with whom Moscow could talk and especially one who would no longer be an instrument in the hands of the West.

"These points were expressed to the Swiss chargé d'affaires with such emphasis that, to my mind, the department deserves to be notified."

MAE/Série EU 1949–1955 Allemagne, Série 4, Soussérie 16, Dossier 6: Russie-Allemagne, 1 July 1949–31 March 1952. Telegram no. 3910/12, Confidential; Distribution List: President of the Republic, President of the Council, Parodi, de la Tournelle, de Bourbon-Busset, Beck.

28. *FRUS 1951* 3:1824.

29. O. Harvey in Paris to the Foreign Office, November 12, 1951. PRO, FO 371/93367/C 1019/262. Record of a conversation with the French Foreign Minister and Maurice Schumann on the proposal for a United Nations commission to investigate conditions in Germany with a view to free elections. Telegram

No. 641, Priority, Secret, "Particular Secrecy," Foreign Office and Whitehall Distribution.

30. See Richard Löwenthal, *Vom Kalten Krieg zur Ostpolitik* (Stuttgart, 1974), p. 14.

31. *Beziehungen DDR-UdSSR 1949 bis 1955: Dokumentensammlung*, 1st half volume (Berlin [GDR], 1975), pp. 338ff.

4. London, Paris, and the First Note

1. Note from W. D. Allen, Foreign Office ("Soviet Government's Note on a German Peace Treaty "), March 11, 1952, with annotations by F. Roberts. PRO, FO 371/97877/C 1074/13.

2. Konrad Adenauer, *Erinnerungen* (Stuttgart, 1966), 2:87.

3. *Frankfurter Allgemeine Zeitung*, March 10, 1982.

4. Hans-Peter Schwarz, ed., *Rhöndorfer Gespräche* (Stuttgart, 1982), 5:54.

5. Interview with Sir Frank Roberts on February 7, 1985, in London.

6. PRO, CAB 128/24. Secret. C.C. (52) 29th Conclusions; conclusions of a meeting of the Cabinet held at 10 Downing Street, S.W. 1, on Wednesday, 12 March 1952, at 11 A.M.; Minute 4.

7. A Eden to the British ambassadors in Washington and Paris, March 12, 1952. PRO, FO 371/97877/C 1074/1. Telegram No. 1110 (Washington), Nr. 295 (Paris), Immediate, Secret, "Particular Secrecy," Foreign Office and Whitehall Distribution.

8. O. Harvey in Paris to A. Eden, March 12, 1952. PRO, FO 371/97877/C 1074/4. Telegram No. 144, Immediate, Secret, "Particular Secrecy," Foreign Office and Whitehall Distribution.

9. On March 13, 1952, the three Western powers gave the Soviet Union a draft of a "shortened" State Treaty with Austria that consisted of a preamble and eight articles. According to this draft, the four occupying powers pledged to withdraw from Austria within ninety days after the treaty came into effect and, most important, to leave to Austria all the assets that had previously been claimed as "German property." This provision affected primarily the Soviet Union. Stourzh believes that this initiative probably "was aimed more toward propagandistic success than toward realistic results," since one could not expect the Soviet Union to sign a treaty that, among other things, again revoked their vested rights to "German property" and did not contain any military provisos (Gerald Stourzh, *Kleine Geschichte des österreichischen Staatsvertrags* [Graz, 1975], p. 220). As was to be expected, the Soviet Union rejected any negotiations concerning this "shortened State Treaty."

10. O. Harvey in Paris to A. Eden, March 13, 1952. PRO, FO 371/97877/C 1074/10. Telegram No. 149, Immediate, Secret, "Particular Secrecy," Foreign Office and Whitehall Distribution.

11. Attitude of the Quai d'Orsay. Note from Frank Roberts, Foreign Office, March 14, 1952, with annotation by A. Eden. PRO, FO 371/97878/C 1074/27.

12. Note from March 15, 1952. FO 371/97877/C 1074/24.

13. DoS 662.001/3-1952; also in Hermann Graml, "Die Legende von der verpaßten Gelegenheit: Zur sowjetischen Notenkampagne des Jahres 1952," *Vierteljahrshefte für Zeitgeschichte* (1981), 29:327.

14. Note from Frank Roberts for A. Eden and W. Strang, "Soviet Note on Germany", March 15, 1952, with commentary by Strang and marginal comments by Eden. PRO, FO 371/97879/C 1074/52.

15. A. Gascoigne in Moscow to A. Eden, March 14, 1952, with commentaries from Hall, Allen, Hobbly, and Roberts as well as annotations by Eden. PRO, FO 371/97877/C 1074/11. Telegram No. 104, Immediate, Secret, "Particular Secrecy," Foreign Office and Whitehall Distribution.

16. I. Kirkpatrick in Wahnerheide to the Foreign Office, March 17, 1952. PRO, FO 371/97878/C 1074/20. Telegram No. 298, Priority, Confidential, Foreign Office and Whitehall Distribution. See Document 5.

17. O. Harvey in Paris to the Foreign Office, March 21, 1952. PRO, FO 371/97879/C 1074/37. Telegram No. 172, Immediate, Secret, Foreign Office and Whitehall Distribution. Also Harvey to the Foreign Office, March 22, 1952. FO 371/97879/C 1074/42. Telegram No. 178, Immediate, Secret.

5. Washington and the First Note

1. See H. A. Byroade to P. Laukhuff concerning his talk with Hallstein. DoS 611.61A/3-1252.

2. Konrad Adenauer, *Erinnerungen* (Stuttgart, 1966), 2:74.

3. O. Franks in Washington to A. Eden, March 13, 1952. PRO, FO 371/97877/C 1074/9. Telegram No. 660, Immediate, Secret, "Particular Secrecy," Foreign Office and Whitehall Distribution.

4. J. McCloy in Bonn to D. Acheson, March 11, 1952. DoS 662.001/3-1152. Incoming Telegram No. 1932 from Bonn, Priority, Confidential.

5. Ibid.

6. "Initial German Reactions to Soviet Tripartite Notes of March 10, 1952." Received at the State Department, March 14, 1952. DoS 662.001/3-1252.

7. J. McCloy in Bonn to D. Acheson, March 12, 1952. DoS 662.001/3-1252. Incoming Telegram No. 1939 from Bonn, Priority, Secret. See Document 1.

8. C. Lyon in Berlin to D. Acheson, March 15, 1952. DoS 662.001/3-1552. Incoming Telegram No. 1139 from Berlin, Confidential Secruity Information. See Document 3.

9. C. Lyon in Berlin to D. Acheson, March 18, 1952. DoS 662.001/3-1852. Incoming Telegram No. 1147 from Berlin, Secret.

10. See chapter 1.

11. J. McCloy in Bonn to D. Acheson, March 16, 1952. DoS 662.001/3-1652. Incoming Telegram No. 1998 from Bonn, Priority, Secret.

12. H. Cumming in Moscow to D. Acheson, March 16, 1952. DoS 662.001/3-1652. Incoming Telegram No. 1479, Priority, Secret. *FRUS 1952–1954*, vol. 7, Document No. 70.

13. P. Laukhuff to American Embassy in London, March 14, 1952. DoS 662.001/3-1432. Outgoing Telegram No. 4510, Secret.

14. Note from W. D. Allen, March 13, 1952. PRO, FO 371/97877/C 1074/1.

15. Memorandum from J. H. Ferguson, Policy Planning Staff of the U.S. State Department, for D. Acheson, March 18, 1952. DoS 662.001/3-1852. Top Secret, Security Information. See Document 2.

16. P. Bonsal in Paris to Dean Acheson, March 20, 1952. DoS 662.001/3-2052. Incoming Telegram No. 5715 from Paris, Secret.

6. Opposition to Reunification in the State Department: March 25–April 9

1. Text in *Department of State Bulletin* (April 7, 1952), 26:530–531.

2. Report from J. Titchener, British embassy in Moscow, March 25, 1952. PRO, FO 371/97880/C 1074/49. Telegram No. 131, Priority, Confidential. The discussion with Cumming, the American chargé d'affaires, took place in an "entirely relaxed" atmosphere (H. Cumming in Moscow to D. Acheson, March 25, 1952. DoS 662.001/3-2552.). Hermann Graml, "Die Legende von der verpaßten Gelegenheit: Zur sowjetischen Notenkampagne des Jahres 1952," *Vierteljahrshefte für Zeitgeschichte* (1981), 29:329, reports on this, and Gerhard Wettig, "Die sowjetische Deutschland-Note vom 10. März 1952: Wiedervereinigungsangebot oder Propagandaaktion?" *Deutschland Archiv* (1982), 2:147, refers to Graml's article and then interprets this as follows: Vyshinskii showed himself to be "quite satisfied that the Soviet proposal for a conference was rejected." And thus are the facts turned upside down!

3. A. Eden to O. Harvey in Paris, March 26, 1952. PRO, FO 371/97879/C 1074/57. Telegram No. 299, Confidential.

4. H. Cumming in Moscow to D. Acheson, March 28, 1952. DoS 662.001/3-2852. Incoming Telegram No. 1548 from Moscow, Priority, Secret, Security Information.

5. C. Steel in Washington to F. Roberts, Foreign Office, April 3, 1952. PRO, FO 371/97881/C 10144/6. Secret.

6. J. McCloy in Bonn to D. Acheson, March 29, 1952. DoS 662.001/3-2952. Incoming Telegram No. 2189 from Bonn, Priority, Secret.

7. J. McCloy in Bonn to D. Acheson, March 29, 1952. DoS 662.001/3-2952. Incoming Telegram No. 2188 from Bonn, Priority, Secret. See Document 8.

8. Memorandum from John H. Ferguson, Policy Planning Staff of the U.S. State Department, March 27, 1952. DoS 662.001/3-2752. Top Secret, Security Information. See Document 7.

9. Note from Louis H. Pollak concerning a discussion in the State Department, April 1, 1952. DoS 662.001/4-252. Department of State, Office of the Secretary, Secret Security Information. *FRUS 1952–1954*, vol. 7, Document No. 81.

10. Two posters are included in Rolf Steininger, *Deutsche Geschichte 1945–1961: Darstellung und Dokumente in zwei Bänden* (Frankfurt, 1983; 5th ed. 1989), pp. 173, 412.

11. Document from April 12, 1952 to Eden. FO 371/97742/C 1017/159. *FRUS 1952–1954*, vol. 7, Document No. 16.

7. The Second Soviet Note, April 9, 1952

1. "Soviet Note of April 9," *Department of State Bulletin* (May 26, 1952), 26:819. *FRUS 1952–1954*, vol. 7, Document No. 82.

2. P. Grey in Moscow to the Foreign Office, April 10, 1952. PRO, FO 371/97880/C 1074/730. Telegram No. 184, Priority, Secret, Foreign Office and Whitehall Distribution. However, a few days later Deputy Soviet Foreign Minister V. A. Zorin spoke to American journalists in Moscow. On April 18, the French embassy in Moscow reported this event to Paris; Zorin apparently expressed Stalin's thoughts. If chances for peace were not to be reduced, then, in his opinion, Germany should not become integrated into the West; this was the content of the Soviet proposals from April 9. From this, Chataigneau, the representative of the French embassy concluded: "The emphasis that Mr. Vyshinskii placed on the final sentence of the Soviet note and Mr. Zorin's comments reveal the Moscow government's determination to integrate East Germany into the Eastern bloc if West Germany should join the Western bloc, that is, if the proposal for unity is not accepted now. To put this another way, Germany will remain divided until a war provides an opportunity for unity to be restored. However eager the USSR is to preserve its domination over the part of Germany that it possesses—even to integrate this part of Germany into its political, economic, and military system—nonetheless this would not prevent the USSR from coming to terms with a united Germany and from thus finding possibilities for diplomatic maneuvering. . . . The Soviet initiative leans toward the considerations of Mr. Aneurin Bevan's supporters and attempts to win over the neutralists on the continent. If its proposal is rejected, the Soviet Union will make the Western allies responsible for the continuing division of Germany, a move that will earn them sympathy from the Germans. The Soviet initiative can be truly accepted by the three Western powers only when the Soviet Union agrees to come to an understanding with them about the prerequisites for organizing and holding free elections and about accepting the results of the elections." Chataigneau, French embassy Moscow, to Quai d'Orsay, April 18, 1952. Telegram No. 935/42, Confidential. MAE/Série EU 1949–1955 Allemagne, Série 4, Sousserie 16, Dossier 6: URSS-Allemagne, 1 April 1952–31 March 1953.

3. P. Grey in Moscow to P. Mason, Foreign Office, April 11, 1952. PRO, FO 371/97881/C 1074/91, Secret.

4. Notes from A. Brooke Turner, Foreign Office, on the Soviet note from April 9, 1952, dated April 10, 1952. PRO, FO 371/97880/C 1074/71.

5. J. McCloy in Bonn to D. Acheson, April 12, 1952. DoS 662.001/4-1252. Incoming Telegram No. 2368 from Bonn, Secret. *FRUS 1952–1954*, vol. 7, Document No. 85.

6. Note from F. Roberts, Foreign Office, April 15, 1952. PRO, FO 371/97880/C 1074/72, Secret.

7. I. Kirkpatrick in Wahnerheide to the Foreign Office, April 16 and 17, 1952. PRO, FO 371/97881/C 1074/81. Telegram No. 380, Priority, Confidential, Foreign Office and Whitehall Distribution. Adenauer described this discussion in detail in his *Erinnerungen* (Stuttgart, 1966), 2:91ff. See Document 9.

8. Kurt Schumacher to Konrad Adenauer, April 22, 1952. Reprinted in Adenauer, *Erinnerungen* 2:84ff.

9. Adenauer's interview with Ernst Friedländer on Northwest German Radio, April 24, 1952; quoted according to the *Bulletin des Presse- und Informationsamtes der Bundesregierung*, April 26, 1952. The interview continues: "When I speak of politics in a larger context, then I certainly do not mean that Germany should itself have a policy for the Eastern region or any sort of regional policy at all. We ourselves have two goals: a united Germany and a united states of Europe, to start with just a nucleus of Europe. Eastern regional policy, world policy—*these are not Germany's concerns*. But these are the *concerns of the world powers*, especially of the United States of America. Within the framework of this world policy, we can certainly count on the time coming, even for the Soviets, when they will need and thus will want to give preference to peace and disarmament over the cold war and the eternal arms race. Not too much imagination is required to envision what might be considered compensatory transactions in exchange for German unity in peace within such a framework." For an English-language summation of Adenauer's interview, see I. Kirkpatrick in Wahnerheide to the Foreign Office, April 25, 1952. PRO FO 371/97881/C 1074/98. Telegram No. 414.

10. U.K. High Commission to the Foreign Office. FO 371/97882/C 1074/117.

11. Kurt Klotzbach, *Der Weg zur Staatspartei: Programmatik, praktische Politik und Organisation der deutschen Sozialdemokratie 1945 bis 1966* (Berlin, 1982), p. 232.

12. Adenauer, *Erinnerungen* 2:87.

13. Memorandum of the U.S. State Department, April 16, 1952. PRO, FO 371/97735/C 1016/83, Secret.

14. Commentary on the U.S. memorandum (Memorandum of the U.S. State Department, April 16, 1952. PRO, FO 371/97735/C 1016/83, Secret.) by J. H. Moore and J. W. Nicholls, British Foreign Office, April 17 and 18, 1952.

15. I. Kirkpatrick in Wahnerheide to F. Roberts, Foreign Office, April 26, 1952. PRO, FO 371/97882/C 1074/108, Confidential.

16. Eden's instructions following the discussion between representatives of the three Western powers in London on April 23, 1952. FO 371/97881/C 1074/102. (Also see Commentary from W. Strang [April 26, 1952] and A. Eden [April 28, 1952] on British Draft of the Western Powers Response Note, April 26, 1952. PRO, FO 371/97882/C 1074/113, Secret.)

17. O. Harvey in Paris to the Foreign Office, April 19, 1952. PRO, FO 371/97881/C 1074/83. Telegram No. 230, Secret, Foreign Office and Whitehall Distribution.

18. Vincent Auriol to Antoine Pinay, April 11, 1952. MAE, Papiers d'Agents, Fonds Robert Schuman, dossier "Allemagne." Passages underlined in text are printed in italic here.

19. J. Dunn in Paris to D. Acheson, April 15, 1952. DoS 662.001/4-1552. Incoming Telegram No. 6330 from Paris, Secret.

20. Secret File, DoS 662.001/4-1152.

21. D. Acheson to the U.S. embassy in London, April 30, 1952. DoS 662.001/4-2552. Outgoing Telegram No. 5592 to American Embassy London, Secret. *FRUS 1952–1954*, vol. 7, Document No. 90.

22. J. McCloy in Bonn to D. Acheson, May 2, 1952. DoS 662.001/5-252. Incoming Telegram No. 2639 from Bonn, Priority, Secret. *FRUS 1952–1954*, vol. 7, Document No. 92.

23. J. McCloy in Bonn to D. Acheson, May 3, 1952. DoS 662.001/5-352. Incoming Telegram No. 2649 from Bonn, Priority, Secret. See Document 10.

24. Adenauer, *Erinnerungen* 2:86f.

25. J. McCloy in Bonn to D. Acheson, May 2, 1952. DoS 662.001/5-252. Incoming Telegram No. 2639 from Bonn, Priority, Secret. *FRUS 1952–1954*, vol. 7, Document No. 92.

26. I. Kirkpatrick in Wahnerheide to the Foreign Office, May 2, 1952. PRO, FO 371/97882/C 1074/115. Telegram No. 455 from Wahnerheide, Immediate, Secret, "Particular Secrecy," Foreign Office and Whitehall Distribution.

27. Foreign Minister R. Schuman to A. Eden, May 6, 1952. PRO, FO 371/97883/C 1074/142. Three days earlier, Massigli reported to the Quai d'Orsay from London: "A few days ago, I had the opportunity to meet a British journalist of the first order who had just returned from Bonn where he had spoken with the chancellor and numerous politicians. He summarized his impressions as follows: 'From the bottom of his heart, Chancellor Adenauer desired nothing more than to maintain the division of Germany and to integrate West Germany into Europe. I am convinced of this. But I return with the equally strong belief that the current pushing German public opinion toward unity will pull him along with it.'" MAE/Série EU 1949–1955 Allemagne, Série 4, Sousserie 6, Dossier 6: Allemagne, Relations entre l'Allemagne occidentale et l'Allemagne orientale, 1 November 1951–30 September 1952. Telegram no. 1990, May 2, 1952, Distribution List: President of the Republic, President of the Council, Parodi, de la Tournelle, de Bourbon-Busset, Beck.

28. W. Gifford in London to Dean Acheson, May 7, 1952. DoS 662.001/5-752. Incoming Telegram No. 5062, Secret.

29. Adenauer, *Erinnerungen* 2:265.
30. DoS 762.00/6-552. May 14, 1952. Department of State, Office of Intelligence Research, Intelligence Estimate No. 39, Secret, Prepared by the Estimates Group, Copy N. 64.
31. "The Embassy of the United States to the Soviet Ministry for Foreign Affairs," May 13, 1952. *FRUS 1952–1954* 7:242–247.
32. Richard Löwenthal, *Vom Kalten Krieg zur Ostpolitik* (Stuttgart, 1974), p. 16.
33. See Rolf Steininger, *Deutsche Geschichte 1945–1961: Darstellung und Dokumente in zwei Bänden* (Frankfurt, 1983; 5th ed., 1989), p. 396.
34. Paul Weymar, *Konrad Adenauer: Die autorisierte Biographie* (Munich, 1955), p. 671.
35. Arnulf Baring, *Außenpolitik in Adenauers Kanzlerdemokratie*, 2 vols. (Munich, 1971), 1:280.
36. UP-Interview, SPD, Special Edition, May 17, 1952.
37. *Verhandlungen des Deutschen Bundestages, 1. Wahlperiode 1949, 23.5.1952*, p. 9415A.
38. *Protokoll der II. Parteikonferenz der Sozialistischen Einheitspartei Deutschlands, 9. bis 12. Juli 1952 in Berlin* (Berlin [GDR], 1952), p. 58.

8. End of the Battle of the Notes

1. "The Soviet Ministry for Foreign Affairs to the Embassy of the United States," May 24, 1952, *FRUS 1952–1954*, vol. 7, Document No. 102.
2. Sir A. Gascoigne to the Foreign Office, May 26, 1952. FO 371/97884/C 1074/158.
3. G. F. Kennan in Moscow to D. Acheson, May 25, 1952. DoS 662.001/5-2552. Incoming Telegram No. 1881 from Moscow, Secret. *FRUS 1952–1954*, vol. 7, Document No. 103.
4. As Acheson reported to Eden on May 26, 1952, in Paris. FO 371/97884/C 1074/161.
5. J. McCloy in Bonn to D. Acheson, May 26, 1952. DoS 662.001/5-2652. Incoming Telegram No. 3091 from Bonn, Confidential.
6. Ibid. and S. Reber in Bonn to D. Acheson, May 29, 1952. DoS 662.001/5-2952. Incoming Telegram No. 3167 from Bonn, Confidential. The latter document stated Kraus (CSU), but probably Franz Josef Strauss is meant.
7. Record of Tripartite Conversations at the Quai d'Orsay, Paris, May 28, 1952. PRO, FO 371/97884/C 1074/167.
8. S. Reber in Bonn to D. Acheson, June 2, 1952. DoS 662.001/6-252. Incoming Telegram No. 3182 from Bonn, Priority, Secret. *FRUS 1952–1954*, vol. 7, Document No. 106. McCloy and his deputy Reber considered the first Soviet note from March 10 a serious offer, but not because it contained Moscow's offer to return to the Allied Control Council, as Graml concludes. The Allied Control Council is first mentioned in the third Soviet note. By mistake,

Graml combined the first and third Soviet notes and the respective interpretations from the U.S. High Commission. (Hermann Graml, "Die Legende von der verpaßten Gelegenheit: Zur sowjetischen Notenkampagne des Jahres 1952," *Vierteljahrshefte für Zeitgeschichte* [1981], 29:327.)

9. O. Harvey in Paris to the Foreign Office, June 7, 1952. PRO, FO 371/97884/C 1074/172. Telegram No. 344, Immediate, Confidential, Foreign Office and Whitehall Distribution.

10. The American embassy in Paris to the State Department, June 11, 1952; quoted in Graml, "Die Legende von der verpaßten Gelegenheit," p. 336.

11. Note for D. Acheson, June 12, 1952. DoS 662.001/6-1252, Secret.

12. O. Franks to the Foreign Office, June 19, 1952. FO 371/97886/C 1074/204, Secret. Also compare O. Franks in Washington to the Foreign Office, June 12, 1952. PRO, FO 371/97884/C 1074/186. Telegram No. 1132, Immediate, Secret, "Particular Secrecy," Foreign Office and Whitehall Distribution.

13. Konrad Adenauer, *Erinnerungen* (Stuttgart, 1966), 2:108–122.

14. Frank Roberts to Sir W. Strang, June 25, 1952. FO 371/97887/C 1074/226.

15. I. Kirkpatrick to the Foreign Office, June 25, 1952. FO 371/97886/C 1074/217.

16. Note from Frank Roberts dated June 26, 1952. FO 371/97886/C 1074/225.

17. "Convention on Relations Between the Three Powers and the Federal Republic of Germany," May 26, 1952. *FRUS 1952–1954*, 7:116.

18. Reprinted in Adenauer, *Erinnerungen* 2:112f.

19. Ward to the Foreign Office, July 3, 1952. FO 371/97887/C 1074/236.

20. Parts of this document are reprinted in Josef Foschepoth, ed., *Kalter Krieg und Deutsche Frage: Deutschland im Widerstreit der Mächte 1945–1952* (Göttingen, 1985), p. 376.

21. Ward to the Foreign Office, July 6, 1952. FO 371/97887/C 1074/252.

22. Ward to the Foreign Office, July 7, 1952. FO 371/97888/C 1074/256.

23. Ward to the Foreign Office, July 8, 1952. FO 371/97888/C 1074/263.

24. "The Embassy of the United States to the Soviet Ministry for Foreign Affairs," July 10, 1952. *FRUS 1952–1954*, vol. 7, Document No. 124.

25. Sir A. Gascoigne to the Foreign Office, July 20, 1952. FO 371/97888/C 1074/266.

26. "The Soviet Ministry for Foreign Affairs to the Embassy of the United States," August 23, 1952. *FRUS 1952–1954*, vol. 7, Document No. 125.

27. Sir A. Gascoigne in Moscow to the Foreign Office, August 25, 1952; note from P. F. Hancock, Foreign Office, August 26, 1952. PRO, FO 371/97889/C 1074/285.

28. T. Achilles in Paris to D. Acheson, August 27, 1952. DoS 662.001/8-2752. Incoming Telegram No. 1251 from Paris, Secret.

29. T. Achilles in Paris to D. Acheson, August 30, 1952. DoS 662.001/8-3052. Incoming Telegram No. 1320 from Paris, Secret.

30. "The Embassy of the United States to the Soviet Ministry for Foreign Affairs," September 23, 1952. *FRUS 1952–1954*, vol. 7, Document No. 138.
31. Sir A. Gascoigne to the Foreign Office, September 23, 1952. FO 371/97892/C 1074/349.
32. G. F. Kennan in Moscow to D. Acheson, August 27, 1952. DoS 662.001/8-2752. Incoming Telegram No. 378 from Moscow, Secret. *FRUS 1952–1954*, vol. 7, Document No. 128.
33. D. Acheson to G. F. Kennan, Setpember 2, 1952. DoS 661.001/9–252. Telegram No. 378, Secret.

9. The Stalin Note: A Missed Opportunity

1. Note from H. Groepper to the author, November 3, 1984.
2. Hermann Graml, "Die Legende von der verpaßten Gelegenheit: Zur sowjetischen Notenkampagne des Jahres 1952," *Vierteljahrshefte für Zeitgeschichte* (1981), 29:341.
3. Lord Salisbury to Prime Minister Churchill, August 17, 1953. PM/S/53/286. FO 371/103673, Secret.
4. Note from F. A. Warner, Foreign Office, dated October 2, 1953. FO 371/103683/C 1071/481, Secret.
5. Hans-Peter Schwarz, ed., *Rhöndorfer Gespräche* (Stuttgart, 1982), 5:40.
6. Konrad Adenauer, *Reden 1917–1967: Eine Auswahl*, ed., Hans-Peter Schwarz (Stuttgart, 1975), p. 482.
7. Hans Jürgen Küsters, ed., *Adenauer: Teegespräche 1950–1954* (Berlin, 1984), p. 39.
8. Ibid., 276.
9. Preface to the facsimile edition of the 1952 *Spiegel* (Königstein, 1984).
10. *Die Zeit*, November 30, 1984. Discussion of the book by Jochen Löser and Ulrike Schilling, *Neutralität für Mitteleurope—das Ende der Blöcke* (Munich, 1984).
11. Waldemar Besson, *Die Außenpolitik der Bundesrepublik: Erfahrungen und Maßstäbe* (Munich, 1979), p. 129; Paul Frank, *Entschlüsselte Botschaft: Ein Diplomat macht Inventur* (Stuttgart, 1981), p. 327.
12. Besson, *Die Außenpolitik der Bundesrepublik*, p. 129.
13. "Obstacles to German Unity," July 23, 1952. FO 371/97736/C 1016/97.

10. The Year 1953: Churchill, Adenauer, and Reunification

1. See Rolf Steininger, "Entscheidung am 38. Breitengrad: Die USA und der Korea-Krieg," *Amerikastudien* (1980), 26:45–53.
2. See the foreign policy section of the Republican Party's election platform from July 10, 1952, in *Documents on American Foreign Relations 1952* (New York, 1953), pp. 80–85; partially translated in *Keesing's Archiv 1952*, pp. 3557f.;

Eisenhower's speech from August 25, 1952, in *Keesing's Archiv 1952*, pp. 3625f. On the entire election campaign, see Robert A. Divine, *Foreign Policy and U. S. Presidential Elections: 1952–1960* (New York, 1974).

3. On the "New Look," see John Lewis Gaddis, *Russia, the Soviet Union and the United States* (New York, 1978), pp. 207–213, and John Lewis Gaddis, *Strategies of Containment* (New York, 1982), ch. 5, "Eisenhower, Dulles, and the New Look," especially pp. 127–141.

4. D. C. Watt, "Churchill und der Kalte Krieg: Vortrag vor der Schweizerischen Winston Churchill Stiftung am 19.9.1981," *Schweizer Monatshefte* (1981), special supplement no. 11, pp. 1–24, here p. 17.

5. Lord Moran, *Churchill: The Struggle for Survival 1940–1965* (Boston, 1966).

6. Also see the description in Moran, *Churchill*, pp. 379–385.

7. Harold Macmillan, *Tides of Fortune* (London, 1969), p. 507.

8. Watt, "Churchill und der Kalte Krieg," p. 18.

9. See Moran, *Churchill*, p. 436 and pp. 449ff. On the following, more complete information is provided in Rolf Steininger, "Ein vereintes, unabhängiges Deutschland? Winston Churchill, der Kalte Krieg und die deutsche Frage im Jahre 1953," *Militärgeschichtliche Mitteilungen* (1984), 36:105–144, as well as Josef Foschepoth, "Churchill, Adenauer und die Neutralisierung Deutschlands," *Deutschland Archiv* (1984) 12:1286–1301.

10. Winston Churchill to Dwight D. Eisenhower, March 11, 1953. PRO, PREM 11/422. Telegram No. 171, Foreign Office to United Kingdom Delegation to United Nations, Immediate, Top Secret, Personal and Private.

11. Dwight D. Eisenhower to Winston Churchill, March 12, 1953. PRO, PREM 11/422. Top Secret.

12. Sir A. Gascoigne to the Foreign Office, March 27, 1953. FO 371/106533/ NS 1051/17.

13. H. A. F. Hohler on March 28, 1953. FO 371/106537/NS 1071/40.

14. William Strang on March 28, 1953. FO 371/106537/NS 1071/40.

15. Message from the Prime Minister, telephoned 3:45 p.m. on March 28, 1953. FO 371/106537/NS 1071/41.

16. See Steininger, "Ein vereintes, unabhängiges Deutschland?" pp. 117ff.

17. Dwight D. Eisenhower to Winston Churchill, May 5, 1953. PRO, PREM 11/421.

18. Winston Churchill to Dwight D. Eisenhower, May 4, 1953. PRO, PREM 11/421, Top Secret.

19. Dwight D. Eisenhower to Winston Churchill, May 5, 1953. PRO, PREM 11/421.

20. Winston Churchill to Dwight D. Eisenhower, May 6, 1953. PRO, PREM 11/421. Telegram No. 2019 to Washington, Immediate, Top Secret.

21. Dwight D. Eisenhower to Winston Churchill, May 8, 1953. PREM 11/421.

22. *Parliamentary Debates*, Hansard (May 11, 1953), 515:897.

23. See Steininger, "Ein vereintes, unabhängiges Deutschland?" pp. 117ff.

24. Winston Churchill to Anthony Eden, April 13, 1952. PRO, FO 371/97735/C 1016/80. Prime Minister's Personal Minute, Serial No. 17/235/52, Private and Personal.

25. Winston Churchill to Sir W. Strang, May 25, 1952. FO 371/97884. Prime Minister's Personal Minute, Serial No. M 303/52. Quotation marks in original.

26. *Parliamentary Debates,* Hansard (May 11, 1953), 515:887–902.

27. Memorandum of the Foreign Office concerning a united, neutralized Germany. William Strang to Winston Churchill, May 30, 1952. PRO, PREM 11/449. PM/WS/53/185, Secret.

28. Response from Winston Churchill to William Strang, May 31, 1953. PRO, PREM 11/449.

29. On Adenauer's visit, see his report in his *Erinnerungen* (Stuttgart, 1966), 2:205–208. The impression Churchill made on his German visitor is described by Herbert Blankenhorn, *Verständnis und Verständigung: Blätter eines politischen Tagebuches 1949–1979* (Berlin, 1980), pp. 150f.; see also Steininger, "Ein vereintes, unabhängiges Deutschland?" p. 129.

30. Adenauer, *Erinnerungen* 2:217f.

31. This five-point program included (1) holding free elections throughout Germany, (2) forming a free government throughout Germany, (3) concluding a peace treaty that would be willingly accepted by this government, (4) settling all remaining territorial questions in this peace treaty, and (5) safeguarding the right of an all-German parliament and an all-German government to negotiate freely within the framework of the principles and goals of the United Nations. Text contained in Heinrich Siegler, ed., *Dokumentation zur Deutschlandfrage* (Bonn, 1961), p. 172.

32. Part of the protest note read as follows: "We condemn the irresponsible resort to military force, which has led to the death or serious injury of a considerable number of citizens of Berlin, including residents of our sectors. We protest the arbitrary measures of the Soviet authorities that have interrupted traffic between the sectors and have restricted the freedom of movement throughout Berlin." Text of the note contained in Bundesministerium für gesamtdeutsche Fragen, ed., *Der Volksaufstand vom 17. Juni 1953* (Bonn, 1953), p. 84.

33. Winston Churchill to William Strang, June 19, 1953. FO 371/103842/CS 1016/124. Prime Minister's Personal Minute, Serial No. M 215/53.

34. The complete document appears in Steininger, "Ein vereintes, unabhängiges Deutschland?" pp. 130f.

35. Ibid., 131–136.

36. Memorandum from Winston Churchill concerning the European Defense Community and the German Question, July 6, 1953. PRO, PREM 11/449.

37. See Steininger, "Ein vereintes, unabhängiges Deutschland?" pp. 121f.

38. According to Minister of the Exchequer Richard Butler in the cabinet meeting of July 13, 1953. CAB 128/26.

39. Moran, *Churchill*, p. 459.

40. Kirkpatrick to the Foreign Office, April 1, 1953. FO 371/103848/CS 1017/6.

41. At least this is what Lord Salisbury reported to Churchill after returning from Washington; see Watt, "Churchill und der Kalte Krieg," p. 19, who refers to an interview with Sir John Colville.

42. Moran, *Churchill*, p. 459.

43. According to the report of Heinz Brandt—Berlin district secretary of the SED at that time—who took refuge in the Federal Republic after June 17, was then abducted by the State Security Police of the GDR, and finally released in 1964 after three years in prison. See his book, *Ein Traum, der nicht entführbar ist* (Munich, 1967), especially pp. 209–223. Richard Löwenthal also refers to this in his introduction to Arnulf Baring, *Der 17. Juni 1953*, 3d ed. (Stuttgart, 1983), p. 18.

44. Richard Löwenthal, *Vom Kalten Krieg zur Ostpolitik* (Stuttgart, 1974), p. 20.

45. Even immediately before and after the Paris Treaties were ratified in 1955 (guaranteeing sovereignty and entry into NATO), the Soviet Union indicated its willingness to discuss this question. (This information kindly provided on November 3, 1984, by the former German ambassador to Moscow, H. Groepper, who refers to a discussion with Ambassador Semenov at the Soviet embassy in Vienna in 1955.) See also Heinrich Krone's diary entries from June 10 and 30, 1955, in Klaus Gotto, *Neue Dokumente zur Deutschland- und Ostpolitik Adenauers*, vol. 3 of *Adenauer-Studien*, eds. Rudolf Morsey and Konrad Repgen (Mainz, 1974), pp. 139f.

46. See Carola Stern, *Ulbricht* (Cologne, 1963), p. 180.

47. See Löwenthal, *Vom Kalten Krieg zur Ostpolitik*, p. 20.

48. Löwenthal in his introduction to Baring, *Der 17. Juni 1953*, p. 15.

1. Hans-Peter Schwarz, *Die Ära Adenauer 1957–1963*, vol. 3 of *Geschichte der Bundesrepublik Deutschland* (Stuttgart, 1983), p. 374.

2. Ibid.

3. Carlo Schmid, *Erinnerungen* (Bern, 1979), p. 527.

4. On October 9, 1952, at a meeting of the Parliamentary Committee for All-German Questions, Undersecretary Hallstein made a statement in principle concerning the issue of reunification: "As far as Soviet Russia's position is concerned, every possibility that assumes a more positive *Soviet outlook concerning reunification* derives from the hypothesis that Soviet Russia has not decided under all circumstances to bolshevize all of Germany. Undersecretary Hallstein explained that this way of thinking cannot be taken for granted. . . . The thought of reunification under conditions of freedom excludes identifying with the Soviet Union's interest in domination. The other question is whether

the Soviet Union can be won over at a price we can pay. Undersecretary Hallstein felt himself compelled at this point to examine the basics of the *problem of a price.* He explained that he was concerned by the candor with which the *problem of [paying] a price to the Soviet Union* was discussed at all. The habit had become established of speaking of this price as a foregone conclusion, which was not at all the case. He was under no illusions; in politics there were situations in which one must soberly consider the facts. But in principle and politically it was incorrect to act as though the Soviet Union had a right to demand a price for releasing a territory it had captured. We would not permit this to happen. We must firmly adhere to the principle that what we are demanding belongs to us" (emphasis in original). Politisches Archiv des Auswärtigen Amts, Bonn, 202–06II

5. December 5, 1953; *FRUS 1952–1954* 5(2):1783.

6. Quoted in Andreas Hillgruber, *Europa in der Weltpolitik (1945–1963)* (Munich, 1981), p. 70. Compare Rolf Steininger, "Das Scheitern der EVG und der Beitritt der Bundesrepublik zur NATO," *Aus Politik und Zeitgeschichte* (April 27, 1985), B 17/85:3–18.

7. In addition to the examples already referred to, a discussion between the long-time French foreign minister, Georges Bidault, and the British ambassador to Paris, Sir Oliver Harvey, should be mentioned. At the end of June 1953, Bidault told Harvey that a united Germany would be incompatible with the European Defense Community, in other words: "The E.D.C. and Western integration are dependent on the maintenance of a divided Germany." Harvey replied that this was "heresy"; everyone, including Adenauer and the French government, had publicly and always with fervor expresssed their support for reunification; but he could not shake the feeling that this was precisely what the French feared the most. He, too, found it difficult to imagine a united Germany with sixty or seventy million inhabitants as a member of the European Defense Community. If this were to occur, France and the other members would be in a hopeless minority. On the other hand, a united Germany would mean the end of Adenauer and the CDU majority and would bring to power the socialists, who were opposed to integration. Since it was just as unlikely that the Soviet Union would accept the risk of a united Germany as a member of the Western camp, as that the West would accept the risk of a united Germany as a member of the Eastern camp, only two possibilities existed: either a united Germany, neutralized, if not actually demilitarized, and under four-power control or a divided Germany such as existed at present, but where the Western part would be integrated into the Western camp not only temporarily but permanently and where the Eastern part would remain a Russian satellite like Poland. O. Harvey to the Foreign Office, June 29, 1953. FO 371/103666/C 1071/62.

8. CAB 129/76.

9. Note on German unity by Ivone Kirkpatrick, December 16, 1955. FO 371/118254/WG1071/G1374, Top Secret.

10. Klaus Gotto, *Neue Dokumente zur Deutschland-und Ostpolitik Aden-*

auers, vol. 3 of *Adenauer-Studien,* eds. Rudolf Morsey and Konrad Repgen (Mainz, 1974), p. 162.

11. Ibid., 165f.

12. Hans-Peter Schwarz, ed., *Rhöndorfer Gespräche* (Stuttgart, 1982), 5:10.

13. Only 26 percent were opposed. In 1978, the percentage of those in favor was 38 and of those opposed, 34; in 1979: 49/26; in 1980: 47/27; in 1981: 54/24; in 1982: 51/23; and in 1983: 55/22. Conditions for reunification: The GDR was to withdraw from the Warsaw Pact, the Federal Republic from NATO. A reunified Germany was to be allowed to determine its own social system through free elections with secret ballots; neutrality and freedom of alliance were to be guaranteed. See Allensbacher Archiv, IfD-Umfrage 4040, March 1984.

INDEX

Acheson, Dean, 15, 57, 65, 76–77, 82, 84, 87–88, 92, 100, 114

Adenauer, Konrad: and Winston Churchill, 107–10; and defense contribution, 24–28, 40, 45–47, 82; and discussions with Western powers, 29–30, 55–56, 68–69, 88–89; and first Soviet note, 21–32, 48, 50–51, 55–56, 62, 141–45, 151–52, 155–58; and free elections, 44–45, 47–48, 54, 67–69, 119; and neutrality, 3, 10, 24–27, 80, 98; and reunification, xvi, 2, 10, 21–25, 28, 50–51, 96–98, 113–21, 179n31; and second Soviet note, 67–72, 76–77, 81–82; and Social Democratic Party, 69–72; and third Soviet note, 88–92

"Alibi theory," *see* Graml, Hermann

Allen, Denis, 49–50, 97

Arndt, Adolf, 82

Auriol, Vincent, 74–75

Austria, 15–16, 52, 117, 169n9

Baring, Arnulf, 2, 22, 25, 31, 82

Beria, L. P., 4, 102, 111

Berlin Wall, 116, 119

Besson, Waldemar, 45, 99

Bevan, Aneurin, 172n2

Bevin, Ernest, 39, 45

Bidault, Georges, 181n7

Blankenhorn, Herbert, 118, 161n22

Blücher, Franz, 62

Blumenfeld, Erik, 99

Bohlen, Charles, 63–65

Bonn Convention, 3–4, 9, 30, 50, 68, 70, 72, 81–82, 91, 96